The Modern
Ignoramus

V. J. Cole

The Modern Ignoramus by V. J. Cole
Published by V. J. Cole in Chicago, Illinois.
Copyright © 2022 V. J. Cole

Cover Design: PixelatedPeach on Fiverr
Editor: GrammarGal on Fiverr
ISBN: 979-8-9864747-0-0 (paperback)
ISBN: 979-8-9864747-2-4 (hardcover)
ISBN: 979-8-9864747-1-7 (eBook)
Library of Congress Control Number: 2022910808
First Edition

The publisher has used its best endeavors to ensure that the URLs for external websites referred to in this book are correct and active at the time of publication. However, the publisher has no responsibility for the websites and can make no guarantee that a site will remain live or that the content is or will remain available.

Every effort has been made to trace all copyright holders, but if any have been inadvertently overlooked, the publisher will be pleased to include any necessary credits in any subsequent reprint to edition.

To all the individuals
who possess the gift of critical thinking,
and especially to my husband, Mr. Cole,
who has been a great inspiration,
and to my dear friend, Mrs. Clark,
who has been keeping me anchored,
I dedicate this work.

Table of Contents

Prologue

The American public has never before been as divided on public opinion and policies as it is today. It is near impossible to read, watch, or listen to the daily news from a source that isn't attempting to sway your views to the far left or the far right. Moderation is hard to come by. Most of the public isn't even open to discussion of any sort and is hard-set in its values and principles. We have all, in the last few years, had to face a friend or relative who is impossible to talk to about politics or any hot topic of the day: the kinds of people who won't even listen to a different opinion. The world is full of big crybabies who refuse to grow up and take responsibility for their own actions, always blaming someone else for their own misfortunes, often brought upon by no other than themselves. Then there are those who fully embrace every new fad, new discovery, and new theory without examination of their sources, their goals, their methods, their legitimacy, and ultimately the possibility of unforeseen repercussions. Overzealous environmentalism is threatening to deepen the economic disparity between the middle class and the top 0.1 percent with sudden changes in many industries, from energy to utilities, to materials, to consumer goods, etc. Reverse racism, through its communist ideologies, is invading every institution and is seeking to replace meritocracy with equity for all: Deeds no longer matter, only the color of your skin when it happens to be any other color but white.

In this work, we will embark on a philosophical journey of exploration, an analysis, a critique, a commentary, if you will, of the mind of modern man, an attempt to examine his habits, motives, and activities of the extreme kind. The goal is to expose the most important aspects of rottenness in the modern individual and the modern collective. We will also attempt to reveal a correlation between this rottenness of the individual and his tendency to favor ideas that are anti-liberal and anti-democratic. We also will document our observations by referring to psychology, philosophy, and history. Additionally, sound conclusions will be drawn based on empirical evidence, decorated with a healthy number of grievances in the process, and we will present ways in which to engage in the discourse necessary to remedy those issues. The democratic discourse is not a monologue, but a dialogue: it requires a thorough and open-minded examination of facts and concerns while participants provide both praise and criticism.

It is my goal to immerse your brain, my dear reader, into the complexities of the issues we face in our day and age. Life is not as simple as black or white, good or evil—

much of it is made up of gray areas in-between. If only one person would begin to doubt and question the contents and validity of the vast amounts of information we are fed through a screen every day on the topics which I am about to cover, then I may consider my job done. Reason and logic are two qualities we as a species seem to lack, and if I could rekindle the flame that is dormant in just one person, then I may rest easy.

Nature of the Beast

Times are bad. Children no longer obey their parents, and everyone is writing a book.

—Marcus T. Cicero

T his quote by the renowned Roman scholar Cicero is just as relevant today as it was in his day in the first century BC. It would seem that no period throughout history is left unscarred by crises worthy of mention by writers, historians, and philosophers, and today is no different. Infantilism, social media, climate change, and ideological conflicts are some of those very crises our society is facing. In what is my first work, we will attempt to analyze and decipher the intricacies of these subjects, some of which are hotly debated and some of which are regrettably ignored by many, so that we, as a country, may continue the liberal and civil progress that the United States was founded upon. We will together trace the roots of these phenomena, analyze the impacts they are having on the individual and the collective, and through rational thinking suggest reasonable actions we may take to mitigate their negative influences.

Let us begin by exploring the very nature of the psyche of modern man and dissect all of the drives which force him to do what he does and how he does it.

The Baby King

The children of today are raised on a pedestal. They cannot be kept without entertainment, they cannot be denied their every whim, and if one dares to discipline their child, they risk dealing with social services. Therefore, children tend to reach maturity at a very late stage in life, all too late for some, through a rude awakening or series thereof. They become whining adults, always expecting things to go their way, and if they don't go their way, then they pout and complain until they get what they want. They do not know or have not learned that life isn't easy, that it isn't always fair, and that Mommy and Daddy won't always be there for them.

In the United States, on average, it is uncommon to come across a family with more than two children.[1] It is perhaps because of this tendency that every child is so precious to their parents, that parents create shields around their young—sort of a bubble between the precious little younglings and the brutality of the world. Parents, by being overly protective, prevent their children from learning real-world lessons and how to handle themselves after they leave the home nest. Like birds with

---

[1] Statista. "Average Number of Own Children Under 18 in Families with Children in the United States from 1960 to 2020." Dec 2020. https://www.statista.com/statistics/718084/average-number-of-own-children-per-family/ Accessed 02/13/2022

no wings, they try to fly off into the world only to realize that things out in the wild are not as rosy as they seem.

Despite having come of age, within the common framework of age progression (child, adolescent, adult), newly formed adults are less and less keen on taking responsibility and being held accountable for the things they do and the consequences that follow. Overly protective parenting and degradation of the education system are some of the causes of what is referred to as *infantilism*. Carl Jung (1875–1961) described this phenomenon from a psychoanalytical frame of reference as the *eternal boy archetype—puer aeternus*—the adult who avoids responsibility,[2] the man-child who understands that adulthood beckons but refuses to grow up and instead waits for somebody else to solve his existential dilemmas. (This can also apply to females, the *puella aeterna*.) An alternative definition of the infantilist enigma could be illustrated as the process of becoming an adult with the attributes and privileges of a child.[3] The children of yesterday—the adults of today—keep on living their lives thinking that no matter what they do, someone will be there to clean up their mess, make their bed, earn them a living, and so on. They lack responsibility, rationale, critical thinking, humility, self-control, self-reflection, and the ability to form personal and professional relationships—

---

[2] Jung, Carl. "The Archetypes and The Collective Unconscious" (*Collected Works of C. G. Jung Vol. 9 Part 1*). Princeton University Press. 1981. pp. 150-160.
[3] Bruckner, Pascal. *The Temptation of Innocence: Living in the Age of Entitlement*. Algora Publishing. 2000. p. 9.

all the traits of maturity. They bear the same attributes of, say, a five-year-old in the body of twenty-some- or even thirty-some-year-olds.

To better understand the psychological condition that is infantilism and how it manifests in society and seeks to shape it, let us begin by referring to one of the greatest minds of the twentieth century, Dr. Sigmund Freud (1856–1939). His contributions to modern psychology are enormous for the simple fact that he examined the human mind to its very depths in extraordinary detail, with many of his methods still in use today. Freud concluded that there are three aspects to a human personality: the id, the ego, and the ego-ideal. *Homo sapiens* infants are only born with an *id*, which comprises the instincts to satisfy one's biological needs for survival (hunger, thirst, comfort) and to please one's senses.[4] As the infant progresses into (biological) adulthood, the person's *ego* is formed—the conscious awareness component of one's personality, which imposes control over the id and its primal needs and desires for the person to behave in a socially accepted manner.[5] The id is the irrational element of one's psyche, whereas the ego is the rational part.

The irrational behaviors exhibited by adults must have a source, and we should attempt to locate it. It is

---

[4] Freud, Sigmund. "The Ego and the Id" *(The Standard Edition of the Complete Psychological Works of Sigmund Freud)*. W. W. Norton & Company. 1990. pp. 8, 17-19.
[5] Ibid.

appropriate to get ourselves acquainted with the Peter
Pan syndrome, a synonym for the puer aeternus, which is
more widely recognized in the United States (*kidult* being
a similar term). Psychologists note that the Peter Pan syndrome is not a psychological disorder, but they do believe that overly protective parenting does children a dis-
service in helping them to confront reality.[6] The Peter
Pans of today see the world as too complicated, too
problematic, and they insist on remaining in a carefree
state, grown-ups with the mentality and entitlement of
children. A fine example of overly protective parenting is
the motto "safety first." A child cannot learn how to ride
a bike without being covered top to toe in protective
gear: helmets, elbow pads, knee pads, reflective coats,
training wheels, and even a very clever invention I re-
cently discovered—a helmet that functions as the automobile's airbag but around your head. I would certainly
understand the extremity in safety gear if one were to let
their young child learn how to ride a bike on a busy Chicago street, but the truth is that parents usually pick a
place where moving vehicles aren't present. The most
preferred place for kids to learn how to bike is the quiet
suburban street where traffic is low and the possibility of
serious injury is extremely low. When I was growing up
thirty years ago, all my peers and I had our knees bruised

---

[6] University of Granada. Overprotecting Parents Can Lead Children to Develop 'Peter Pan Syndrome.' ScienceDaily. www.sciencedaily.com/re-
leases/2007/05/070501112023.htm. Accessed 06/06/2022.

when we failed to keep balance the first couple of times we got on bikes. It would pain me to see my child with a bruised knee, but it also isn't the end of the world, and it acts as a motivation of sorts to focus on balance.

Another fantastical paradox in regard to child safety is that children genuinely do not know how to cross the street. Parents and teachers prefer to rely on fancy street signs and flashing lights to allow children to cross, but they are not taught the basics: to always look both ways before crossing, to never cross in front of a large vehicle due to poor visibility, to never cross when a crosswalk isn't present, and so on. This obsession with safety reinforces children's minds with the expectation that others are responsible for their safety. It is never one's own fault but somebody else's.

The child is placed on a pedestal, surrounded by every object their little mind could desire. The child is treated like a king or queen. The child kings and queens are to be adored and glorified beyond measure, without question. Your Majesty the Baby is the supreme being who, by divine exaltation, is entitled to be the ruler of the land, with a bib in the one hand and a smartphone in the other.

Just as a child is entitled to a meal, so are the baby kings *entitled* to everything they need to continue their vegetative state of carelessness, of endless entertainment and comfort. It isn't, however, only the parents' fault for the idolization of the young. The education system has been adapted to accommodate the needs of

Baby Almighty and has thus had a strong influence on the solidification of the new monarch's claims to the throne. No longer is it acceptable for a student to give their best effort; simple participation is good enough. Those that don't make it to the top are given participation trophies in order not to hurt their feelings. Teachers are in the classroom to serve the newly crowned princes and princesses and to ensure their needs are met, i.e., constant satisfaction.

Researchers argue that infantilism is not a trait to be judged and that infantilism could be regarded as a time-difference attribute of personal development.[7] In the age of careless and never-ending entertainment, the baby personality is accepted as the norm, a legitimate way of life; it is considered an alternative life trajectory.[8] I believe that, on the contrary, there is reason to criticize infantilism, as we are about to trace a correlation between the carefree mentality and the tendency to favor extremist, despotic, and anti-democratic ideals. The infantile adult refuses to confront the complexities of life.[9] He wants to be surrounded by ideas and words which he finds within his comfort zone; complex ideas make him feel uncomfortable and offended, and he wishes to be rid

---

[7] Mezentseva, Liudmila. Infantilism as a Norm: Why It Is Worth Rethinking Age Boundaries. EurekAlert. 05/25/2018. https://www.eurekalert.org/news-releases/694961. Accessed 06/06/2022.
[8] Ibid.
[9] "On Political Correctness and Clear Thinking" | Stephen Fry | COMEDY | *The Rubin Report*. 04/04/2016. Video, 11:28. https://youtu.be/eJQHakkViPo.

of them, to erase them from the pages of history, much like babies push an object to the side which they find against their liking. Those who find themselves offended by ideas, which require critical thinking and the platform of free speech and free thinking to analyze, immediately take action to remove any possibility of discourse on those subjects. Higher education facilities, being the business entities that they are, wish to keep their students happy and in turn treat their students as customers, only to bolster the mentality of half-grownups.[10] The college and university campus is a "safe place" meant to protect the emotional and psychological well-being of students.[11] That which students find offensive, they also find emotionally traumatic. Students are not taught *how* to think but what not to say; in other words, they are coerced into *what* to think. What is it that they are taught to think? It is that feelings matter most and that no person should ever have their feelings hurt: "I feel, therefore I am king!"

---

[10] Dnes, Anthony. "We Must Reverse the Infantilization of Higher Education." The James G. Martin Center for Academic Renewal. 03/17/2017. https://www.jamesgmartin.center/2017/03/must-reverse-infantilization-higher-education/ Accessed 06/06/2022.
[11] Myers, Andrew. "The Coddling of the American Mind." *The Atlantic.* Sept 2015. https://www.theatlantic.com/magazine/archive/2015/09/the-coddling-of-the-american-mind/399356/ Accessed 06/06/2022.

Narcissus Almighty

Parents are very good at satiating the baby king within their children: "You are the smartest boy/girl in your school. You are the most handsome, most gifted," and so forth. Even my mother is guilty of this. Indeed, though, wouldn't you as a parent feel the same? Your child is the smartest, most gifted, and most handsome to you because he's your child and not somebody else's, but that isn't reflective of other children. The constant psychological reinforcement of narcissism is having a negative effect on adolescents and is turning them into entitled egomaniacal adults. The blind self-righteousness we raise the young generation with leads to *narcissistic entitlement,* which is characterized by an unrealistic sense of self-importance and produces an unreasonable expectation to be treated favorably without the sense of reciprocality.[12]

Narcissism is a condition of varying degrees that can be measured using the Narcissism Personality Inventory. One of the most common traits that self-absorbed beings exhibit include listening to only dismiss, negate, or ignore someone else's concerns; deflecting negative criticism toward them and the tendency to become angry when

---

[12] Farmer, Sally. "Entitlement in Codependency." *Journal of Addictive Diseases.* 1999. 18:3. p. 56. https://doi.org/10.1300/J069v18n03_06 Accessed 02/14/2022.

criticism is received; feeling their physical and intellectual attributes are above everyone else; blaming others
for things that go wrong. Narcissistic personality traits
may begin to form in the family, but they have a powerful
facilitator—social media. The era of smartphones witnessed the peculiar phenomenon of *selfie queens and kings.*
Allow me to provide you with the indulgence to illustrate
selfie culture with the following scenario. Ms. Self-Important, a dazzling high school personality laden in
kitschy apparel, holds her smartphone up with one hand,
directs it at her face covered in tons of makeup, puckers
her lips in a seductive fashion, makes a provocative
peace sign with the other hand, and snap, snap, snap!
Then her best friend, a loyal and equally magnificent pro-
tégé and courtier, joins in the fun. Many more selfie pictures are taken within a matter of seconds and analyzed
for imperfections, and the best ones are blasted onto social media. Friends and enemies are to marvel at the
beauty of the two goddesses, and potential mates are to
be encountered. Mr. Self-Important, an alpha leader of
the high school pack, comes across the ostentatious display of testosterone-pumping grimaces and bodily exhi-
bitions and is immediately intoxicated. Unable to resist
the spell, his reaction is to grab his own smartphone,
point it at himself, flex his over-pumped glazed muscles,
make a harsh manly frown, and snap! The beta member
of the pack makes a similar fraternal presentation in
front of the camera, and a response is broadcasted. This

fascinating online courtship results in a place and time to be arranged for the godly suitors and divine damsels to engage in a carnal union of beauty and handsomeness, tackiness and boorishness, seduction and savagery—a parody of femininity and masculinity.

Indeed, the dramaturgy of those obsessed with physical appearance is exemplified on various social media outlets so that many more narcissistically leaning individuals may imitate. However, when the attractiveness of the self-loving narcissist is evaluated by independent third parties, the overestimated charm is found to be less attractive and less appealing than those who care about appearance but aren't obsessed with it.[13] The modern narcissist lacks moderation in his or her vanity.

We have two generations of people—millennials and generation Z—who were and are being brought up with a seemingly infinite self-confidence that fails miserably in the inevitable confrontation with reality. A large colorful balloon that is bound to either deflate itself with the passage of time or, what is more likely, to pop loudly by the touch of a needle. The narcissist is the living embodiment of the modern individual. By definition, everything about the narcissist is divine, is of outstanding quality, and cannot simply be any less than extraordinary. Regardless of

---

[13] Re, Daniel; Wang, Sylvia; He, Joyce; Rule, Nicholas. "Selfie Indulgence: Self-Favoring Biases in Perceptions of Selfies." *Social Psychological and Personality Science 7*, no. 6 (August 2016): 588–96. https://doi.org/10.1177/1948550616644299.

one's capabilities, intellect, or skills, the narcissist proclaims that all values he or she holds are superior to all the rest and can't possibly be wrong. "I am; therefore I am better than everyone else!"

Very few are, in actuality, worthy of such worship. Most are simply plain, unimaginative, and dull. They fit together perfectly in a crowd of sheep, herding like-minded individuals into a mob whose purpose is to show the ignorami and the heretics how wrong and far from the truth they are. Research shows that when the Baby Almighty narcissist is placed in a higher education environment, he performs poorly in courses he finds unexpectedly challenging, compared to other students who do not take success for granted.[14] For some, that is the rude awakening to their rosy daydream; others simply continue with their habits down the road.

Since narcissists truly believe they are faultless, they find themselves in an inevitable conflict with the world around them because it could never be their fault, but the entire world's fault. They could never perceive themselves as evil, so they see evil only in others. Narcissus is God's chosen, the messiah sent by divine intervention to cleanse the world of all that is evil. He is capricious, unfathomable, omniscient, omnipotent, and omnipresent;

[14] Anderson, Donna, Halberstadt, Jamin and Aitken, Robert. "Entitlement Attitudes Predict Students' Poor Performance in Challenging Academic Conditions." *International Journal of Higher Education*. 2013. 2:2. p. 158. https://doi.org/10.5430/ijhe.v2n2p151. Accessed 02/13/2022.

his purpose is to cast his righteous verdict on the infidels and wreak havoc and devastation in his wake.

Like birds of a feather, narcissists find each other and unite in their thirst for blood, a swarm of locusts that devours and devastates everything in its path. The narcissistic crowd is not open to discussion or compromise. Their demands must be satisfied because they come from a divine source—the infantile self. Any possibility of meaningful discussion is turned into a barrage of accusations. If you don't agree with the self-righteous narcissistic mob, then you are either racist, misogynist, an idiot, or some other term like it. They are united in ideology, and their purpose is to crush all who oppose their ideas of a perfect world ruled by crybabies. Their zeal goes beyond just snarky online comments. They are social media detectives. If you happen to find yourself holding views that are different from those of the zealous narcissists and dare to express them publicly, they find where you live, where you work, and demand that your employer fires you, because there is no place where the likes of you are welcome. The justice sleuths of the Internet adore costing the livelihoods of people they perceive as enemies. The true goal of the infantile-narcissist ethos of our society is the destruction of free speech and critical thinking—the tyranny of the innocent and self-loving *puer aeternus* and *puella aeterna*.

The Online Sycophant

Due to the nature of our consumerist society, and having been taught no patience when it comes to the acquisition of goods and services, the self-absorbed baby adult is in constant need of instant gratification, entertainment, and satisfaction. We cannot possibly wait for the next big-hit melodrama to air on TV; we must binge-stream it on the day of release! We must have access to all fifty thousand streaming services, racking up hundreds of dollars in subscription fees, lest we miss out on an amazing show that everyone is talking about! We must also pay a yearly fee for the privilege of *two-day free shipping* on every cheap China-made gadget we discover for sale online, and we must also pay *high credit card interest* on these purchases! We must, in addition, keep track of everything that our dear friends post on social media. It would be disgraceful if we didn't have accounts with every single social media website. What's more, we must consume news that is specifically *tailored* to our interests and activities. Every time John Doe posts a silly video of his dog playing the flute, we are shocked by a dinging noise known as a *notification* on our smartphones, marked with a distinct red dot beckoning us to immerse ourselves into the amazing feat that Sir Lancelot the Cur has mustered.

Our cultural decline is total. The deep plunge of intellectual sophistication has reduced a great portion of the population to mindless smart device clickers and couch potatoes. Nobody is interested in literature, poetry, history, philosophy, opera, and theater. The consumer of the twenty-first century consumes so much information online, and yet it is information that is useless to the development of cultural refinement. The consumption of worthless information does not elevate the self above the dull and mundane, but it reinforces the vulgarity and creative degeneration. The information consumer, enslaved by e-commerce, video streaming, and social media, a narcissist and a chronic complainer, is not well versed in the art of critical thinking and is incapable of employing his gray cells to their full capacity.

It is a whole other world out there on the Internet, one that's separate from physical reality but also an extension of our psyche, our most primal desires. The "metaverse" acts as a drug—it stimulates our id and beckons it to satisfy its wants. The need for instant gratification is solidified because the online world cares nothing for the long-term plans we need to make to help our desires become reality. Online advertising seeks to provide (near) immediate satisfaction to our pleasure points with total disregard for rationality and the emotional, economic, and intellectual well-being of individuals.

Artificial intelligence (AI), the algorithms by which all online advertising and suggestion mechanisms are powered, is overwhelming the human brain with a constant volley of things that interest us and cause us to become fixated on them. Addictions are created and reinforced for the sole purpose of keeping us tethered to our smart devices. The exploitation of our psychological predispositions is the primary driver for huge corporate profits that fuel the expansion of this online black hole.

For AI to remain in control, it must also exploit our fears. We are in our conform zone when we're surrounded by the things we know and care about. The thought of the unknown is daunting to us, and we seek to avoid it at all costs. The proverb of the king who judged a criminal[15] is a fine illustration: the criminal was given two options—to be hung by the neck or to take an unknown punishment behind a closed door. The criminal chose the rope, and as the noose was being slipped on him he asked to know what was behind the door. The king told him that his freedom stood behind the door but because most criminals before him usually chose the rope, the king wasn't surprised. AI claims to help us discover new things we may find interest in, but those tend to be the same concepts we are familiar with, only differing in packaging. For those who find no faults within their selves, AI is the fuel for their zeal.

---

[15] Salmansohn, Karen. *How to Be Happy, Dammit: A Cynic's Guide to Spiritual Happiness.* Celestial Arts. 2001. p. 58.

Social media, the partner in crime to advertising and e-commerce where AI pulls the strings, has had a profound influence on the minds of adolescents and adults alike. It has transformed the fabric of society just in the last twenty years. Everybody can post, like, and share whatever interests them, and social media has become an outlet for those who believe the world should bend the knee and bask in their magnificence. Every word is dissected, overly-analyzed, and judged by the standards of Big Tech. The Orwellian definition of misinformation is rampant, it is hunted down zealously and purged from the face of the Internet. The sadistic narcissist shows his true colors on social media and at social justice protests. The narcissistic mob is worshipped and financially incentivized not just by corporate America, but by governmental agencies also: Black Lives Matter, Antifa, Critical Race theorists, and apocalyptic fanatics to name a few beneficiaries. Those who are against them are crucified, just like Jesus is said to have died on the cross for our sins, so must the mob's enemies be eaten alive by scavengers for all the Internet to see.

> Leave no corner of the Internet unturned,
> All so-called fake news must be churned!
> Who dares question leftist wisdom,
> the pinnacle of their Bolshy system?
> Slice and gash and cut those sinful words
> lest misinformation may befall the herds,

with help of mighty brethren of El Chapo
the social fact-check gestapo!

The Afflicted Attention Seeker

It should come as no surprise that the baby kings and queens of today adore to complain in their everyday lives. Social media gives them the perfect outlet to do that. Social media is also their enabler. People are hungry for attention, and they've been granted the best place to get it. It is a psychological condition, a byproduct of the addiction to the online cacophony, a barrage of personalized content and dopamine-inducing smartphone nudges.

Far too many self-proclaimed experts are found on social media, specializing in political, social, and economic forces beyond their academic capacity. They know the exact reasons why inflation is high, gasoline prices skyrocket, and countries go to war, and of course, they know exactly who is to blame. The blame is expressed in the form of *memes*—a picture portraying a scene meant to trigger a personal connection with the audience. The memes also contain short and wise messages which reduce the complexities of those issues to a single person, typically the current president of the United States at the time of publication. Such is the recurring theme of the infantile simpleton: "The president is to blame for everything." The all-knowing infantilist is all too happy to spread their simplicity, which we may define thus: ignorance and gullibility, and consequently the tendency to believe in conspiracy theories and pure propaganda—the bane of social media. If social media is the scourge of its users, its users, in return, are its affliction. However, if social media platforms have the privilege of escaping the consequences of this endless cycle of affliction after continual public scrutiny, its users do not possess this privilege.

What social media giants have known for years has been confirmed: their online platforms are harmful and toxic to youngsters. Social media is to blame for anxiety, depression, and suicidal thoughts,[16] maladies all too common for the younger generation. Social media addiction is leading to and is already causing great concerns in society. For some, it is manifested as a burning hunger for attention, recognition, bragging, bullying, and proving that they are better than everyone else. It synergizes well with the narcissist condition that parents and teachers nurture in children, feeding the flames and egos of the little Narcissus. Eventually what becomes of this malaise? The reality is that many a teenager is prescribed all kinds of antidepressants before they even reach adulthood. In 2019 it is estimated that 10 percent of female teens and 5

---

[16] Wells, Georgia; Horwitz, Jeff; Seetharaman, Deepa. "Facebook Knows Instagram Is Toxic for Teen Girls, Company Documents Show." *The Wall Street Journal.* 2021. https://www.wsj.com/articles/facebook-knows-instagram-is-toxic-for-teen-girls-company-documents-show-11631620739?mod=article_inline Accessed 1/29/2022.

percent of male teens were prescribed antidepressants to treat symptoms of anxiety, depression, or insomnia.[17]

Indeed, too many teenagers and young adults suffer from anxiety. They are fully aware of the complexities of life—which scares them and leads to the formation of insecurities and low self-esteem. Adolescence for them is full of anxiety and fear of the uncertainty of what lies ahead.[18] The thought of leaving the comfort zone of careless existence terrifies them. The cruelty of the world is like adding insult to injury—it not only is a source of anxiety for youngsters but also provides dopamine-triggering methods to reinforce this anxiety. Social media, a scourge for the modern youth as we concluded earlier, does not help youngsters overcome their fears, but it serves to reinforce them and delays their coming of age.[19]

Numerous times there has been established a strong correlation between emotional well-being and low or no social media use.[20] What is it about social media that causes and/or encourages the hunger for self-proof? Is it

---

[17] Elflein, John. *"Antidepressant* Use Among Teenagers in the US from 2015–2019, by Gender." Statista. 07/17/2020. https://www.statista.com/statistics/1133612/antidepressant-use-teenagers-by-gender-us/. Accessed 05/22/2022.

[18] Bernardini, Jacopo. "The Infantilization of the Postmodern Adult and the Figure of Kidult." *Postmodern Openings*. Vol. 5, Issue 2. 2014. pp. 39-55.

[19] Banschick, Mark. "Failure to Launch: The Puer Aeternus: When Adulthood Seems Like Too Much.Psychology" *Today*. 06/11/2021. https://www.psychologytoday.com/au/blog/the-intelligent-divorce/202106/failure-launch-the-puer-aeternus Accessed 06/08/2022

[20] Hunt, Melissa; Marx, Rachel; Lipson, Courtney; Young, Jordyn. "No More FOMO: Limiting Social Media Decreases Loneliness and Depression." *Journal of Social and Clinical Psychology*, Vol. 37, No. 10, 2018, pp. 751-768

the very nature of the beast—an exploiter of low self-confidence? You see your friends' pictures while enjoying their dream vacation, the brand-new luxury car of your boss, or what a blast your ex is having with his or her new-found soul mate. All of these perfect little scenes that you're not a part of, that are out of your grasp, and that you may never experience. Our insecurities lead us on this path to prove to the entire world that we can afford more lavish vacations and more expensive cars, have smarter girlfriends/boyfriends, and so on. We, and our children, have become these petty little fools competing with friends, family, and people we don't care about who has a better life to show off on the Internet. Behind the scenes are the masterminds of these vicious cycles, Big Tech CEOs worth billions of dollars and other clever and not-so-clever technocrats, who are paid by advertisers to flood our news feeds with ads about products we may be interested in, based on the personal information we've willingly provided them. This leads us to wonder how this tale unfolds and who gets the better end of the bargain—the fish or the fisherman?

The Greedy Victim

Our legal system frequently sides with His Majesty, the baby, in what is known as frivolous litigation. When the baby king is wronged in any way, he must employ his manipulator skills to still get his way. The narcissistic infantile is always right and must always be granted every wish. There is a reason a cup of coffee is riddled with large red letters: "Caution! Hot!" If somebody trips and breaks a leg on your driveway, while technically trespassing, they are due millions of dollars in damages. The narcissistic baby-adult does not dial his insolence down even when extreme mass shooting cases are involved—it is not the shooter's fault, but naturally, the parents of the killers, the venues, those who worked at the venues, and even the gun manufacturer's fault who must pay for the shooter's crimes, as if the manufacturer put the gun in the shooter's hands and forced him to massacre dozens of people.

Why is it that the gun manufacturer is to blame? It isn't simply the need to lay blame on somebody else; the underlying factor is money. The shooter, either dead or behind bars, cannot provide the financial windfall that the plaintiffs are looking for, so naturally, whoever's next in line with a deep enough pocket must pay for the crimes of others. Somehow money is to fix the injustices, money is to make us feel like the victims have been brought back to life, that justice has been done. The *monetization of tragedy* has become an industry and a hobby: thirty-six lawsuits following the Columbine shooting were settled for a combined $970 million;[21] $800 million was awarded to victims of the 2017 Las Vegas shooting;[22] lawyers for victims of a concert mass shooting tragedy are seeking $750 million in damages from the performers.[23] The motives behind those lawsuits may be noble and understandable, but in the end, the lives lost are reduced to dollar amounts, aren't they? Are we to drown our sorrows in gold and diamonds as everyday reminders of the cruelty of fate, as scars to be proudly worn and displayed in public? "I've suffered; therefore I deserve to be rich!" Being able to slap a price tag on our agony gives us comfort; it makes the pain subside. At the heart of this atrocious reaction to human anguish is greed, and greed may well bring about the demise of this country. Greed is the major reason why millions of Americans cannot afford

---

[21] ABC News. *"Columbine Families Settle Suits with Parents."* https://abcnews.go.com/US/story?id=93525&page=1. Accessed 06/07/2022.
[22] Rose, Andy; Silverman, Hollie. "A Judge Has Approved an $800 Million Settlement for Victims of the Las Vegas Shooting." CNN. 09/30/2020 https://www.cnn.com/2020/09/30/us/las-vegas-shooting-settlement-approved/index.html. Accessed 06/07/2022.
[23] Morin, Alyssa. "AstroWorld Tragedy: $750 Million Lawsuit Filed Against Travis Scott on Behalf of Victims." E! News. 11/17/2021 https://www.yahoo.com/entertainment/astroworld-tragedy-750-million-lawsuit-231819394.html Accessed 06/07/2022

health insurance.[24] Greed is the major reason millions of diabetics in the United States are forced to pay anywhere between $300 and $700 for a vial of insulin when the same, for example, only costs $65 in Canada.[25] Greed is the major reason Big Tech giants have been keeping hundreds of billions of dollars tucked away in tax-haven countries in the Caribbean,[26] a vast and unimaginable cash hoard of the covetous technocrats, for the mere convenience of avoiding corporate tax. Meanwhile, the Federal government has amassed a staggering $30 trillion in debt, and the amount continues to rise with every passing second. Could the pretentious egotistical baby king be banished so that we may gain control over greed, start taking responsibility, and put our gray cells to work?

Portraying oneself as the victim of circumstance is a classic manipulator's method to gain pity, sympathy, and/or compassion in order to acquire something from

---

[24] Kaplan-Weisman, Laura. "Why Americans Can't Afford Health Care: The History." *Baltimore Sun*. 08/02/2019. https://www.baltimoresun.com/opinion/op-ed/bs-ed-op-0804-medicare-history-20190802-acdj2ebw4ncn7h42rupwlwrcty-story.html. Accessed 06/07/2022.
[25] Howatt, Glenn. "Soaring Insulin Prices Cause Minnesota Lawmakers to Draft Remedies." *Star Tribune*. 12/12/2018. https://www.startribune.com/soaring-insulin-prices-cause-minnesota-lawmakers-to-draft-remedies/502531441/. Accessed 06/07/2022.
[26] Rubin, Richard. "Cash Abroad Rises $206 Billion as Apple to IBM Avoid Tax." *Bloomberg News*. 03/12/2014. https://www.bloomberg.com/news/articles/2014-03-12/cash-abroad-rises-206-billion-as-apple-to-ibm-avoid-tax#xj4y7vzkg. Accessed 06/07/2022.

someone. [27] The entitled-infantilist ethos is the vehicle that allows greed to develop. Greed is an essential characteristic of the big crybabies who have figured out that to get what they want, sometimes they must exploit the *victim card.* The victim-manipulator exploits the consciousness of caring people who cannot stand to see anyone suffering. It has become pathological and idiosyncratic, this constant need to self-victimize oneself, a state of endless torment by the world and its denizens. To describe oneself as a victim is to elevate oneself to a "candidate for exception."[28] In a world full of entitled victims, greed perverts the occurrence of misfortune, and the *trivialization of tragedy* becomes the status quo. Every single misfortune that befalls them is the worst that could ever happen. It is comparable to the worst of history's atrocities, and it must be avenged—monetarily! They cry foul, and everyone must listen and sympathize with them. All branches of media are there to tell the world just how miserable they've become, and somebody or something out there is to blame, naturally—or sometimes, *everybody,* by association! Take this for instance: there are those among us who think that auto insurance companies are

[27] Simon Jr, George. "In Sheep's Clothing: Understanding and Dealing with Manipulative People." A. J. Christopher & Company. 1996. https://www.goodreads.com/work/quotes/367996-in-sheep-s-clothing-understanding-and-dealing-with-manipulative-people. Accessed 01/29/2022.
[28] Bruckner, Pascal. *The Tyranny of Guilt: An Essay on Western Masochism.* Princeton University Press. 2010. p. 142.

now to be held responsible for the transmission of sexually transmitted diseases occurring in vehicles insured by those companies.[29] Such victims deserve sympathy and compassion, but should they be awarded millions of dollars to be paid by entities and people who have no direct reasonable association with the "insured"? Has the infantile's vulgarity spilled into unreasonable demands on society, and has it thus become the new normal—the dynasty of the Eternal Victim?

What underlies the pathos, the tragic existence, of the Eternal Victim exhibited by selfish abuse of the legal system? Behind the sad, injured face lies complexes and insecurities that lead to anger, envy, and jealousy about how other people have done better in life, but they, the self-victimized crybabies, do not want to lift a finger. Their favorite pastime is to complain through their enabler, social media: their meal is cold, somebody doesn't like them, somebody did or said something rude to them, somebody looked at them funny. Through their toxic personalities, such people manage to estrange and banish everyone unlike them from their inner circles. Eventually, when the victims find themselves alone with nobody willing to extend a helping hand, they start to complain to the government. The welfare state is out there to feed

---

[29] Li, David. "Geico Must Pay $5.2 Million to Woman Who Got HPV From Sex in Man's Insured Car, Court Rules." NBC News. 06/09/2022. https://www.nbcnews.com/news/us-news/geico-must-pay-52-million-woman-got-hpv-sex-mans-insured-car-court-rul-rcna32831. Accessed 06/09/2022.

them, to pay for child care, for diapers, for strollers, for baby formula and their children's education; they must be provided food, shelter, a job, and even pocket money—all the necessities of a sustained vegetative existence. The list is endless just as one's needs are endless. You hardly hear the truly homeless and desperate ever complain, but young, able bodies are lining up to get food stamps, baby diapers, and disability parking stickers. Homelessness, for many, is a choice. And the government is all too willing to take care of its people, for a price, of course: "We'll give you more money, but we want some of your freedom in exchange." Long live the new king!

It is those without purpose in life, empty and disheartened, who claw in the dirt and wail in their agony, helpless to take their own destiny by the reigns and forge a path forward. The only purpose in life that they find is to either evoke sympathy and pity or to denounce someone else's evil deeds and swat them like the insects that they are. The infantile victim is always in the right, always knows everything, and cannot be reasoned with. You are either with them or against them.

The narcissistic baby victim has a splendid way to pat himself or herself on the back. When I hear the word *hero* I invoke images of Hercules, Joan of Arc, and even Jesus Christ, for it is a noble story to tell. Two characteristics make a hero—courage and sacrifice—which lead to the performance of an extraordinary feat. An English proverb teaches that "a hero is a man who is afraid to run away," and in the face of doom, a hero acts without hesitation, without the expectation to get something in return, whether it be monetary gain or fame. A hero is also ready and willing to sacrifice themselves for their cause, a cause for the betterment of others. An example of a true hero is the soldier who throws his body over a live grenade to save his fellow soldiers.

In a society governed by infantile victims, martyrdom is their ascent to glory. The victim is hailed as a hero for the betterment of their own, self-absorbed beings. We've all seen the multitude of signs "Heroes Work Here" in the last couple of years—simply showing up to work, to get paid, is considered a trait of heroism. Everyone is a *hero*! Teachers are heroes, parents are heroes, retail workers, truck drivers, farmers, politicians, and caregivers are heroes only because they are doing their job. What is it that is courageous and sacrificial about the jobs of caregivers, cashiers, truck drivers, and teachers? That is not to say that their deeds don't deserve recognition and celebration—on the contrary! They perform a vital task in the functioning of society. However, their deeds do not amount to heroism. Those who sacrifice themselves willingly in the name of the health and education of others may have done a heroic act, but that act is not an extraordinary feat; there are too many of them doing the same thing. Those who yet live are no heroes for simply getting paid for working in a high-risk environment. It's hard to do a job and get paid a salary for it; blaming the world for all the suffering they've endured in the profession they've chosen makes them feel warm and fuzzy inside. A glorification of the irresponsible and self-righteous: "I've suffered; therefore I am a hero!"

The Wanderers

The unquenchable thirst to elevate oneself above all others could also be quantified as the lack of purpose in life, a void that is present in the hearts and seemingly impossible to fill. For a couple of centuries now we have had a society that has severed its connection to the Christian church, a society that used to be extremely devout, has been living without the looming possibilities of ending up in the depths of hell if one sins, or to be reunited with our maker in heaven if we live by his words.

Religion used to give our lives purpose and meaning. Now, faced with all the knowledge we've gathered of the inner workings of the universe, way too many don't know what to do. In our little minds, religion gave us order and science gave us chaos. Religion is dying a slow and agonizing death, and in its absence, people seem unable to find a new purpose. For some, to live a life without a higher purpose, with the realization that there may be no beyond but only a black void and nothingness after death, is to be lost. It is to drift from one thing to another, ever to wander the labyrinths of an unknown, foreign land, and everything that one finds interest in turns into an obsession, an addiction. Like bees, they fly from flower to flower: when one flower is no longer entertaining, they simply hop to the next one that catches their attention, and the next one. Like stray dogs begging for scraps, they hope that something or someone will deliver them from pain and hunger and show them the path to salvation. Their labors have no meaningful and lasting fruit to bear, no tale to tell, no legacy.

In the reflection of the distorted and warped mirror that is fate, we find another band of wanderers—those who reject the harsh truth of life and instead immerse themselves in the utopian worlds of fantasy and sci-fi. Video games, movies, TV shows, novels, comics, and virtual reality technologies seek to teleport those who are disappointed with the real world into universes full of fantastical creatures, wizards, dragons, and superheroes. The escapist is not interested in forging his own reality in the here and now—he denies and denounces its existence. He wishes it weren't real because it's a source of disappointment, grief, and despair. He would rather spend his years of youth in a different world, one that is simpler to understand, one which does not cause him pain, one which doesn't require him to grow up. His body wanders the Earth, but his mind lives in an imaginary place.

More than a century ago, Friedrich Nietzsche (1844–1900) identified the aimlessness that humanity has been facing and suggested a path of salvation; he gave us guidance on how to fill the void—the Übermensch. This superb being is the embodiment of a new human who learns to live outside the boundaries of faith and fantasy, who will forge his own new set of values and elevate himself above the banal, the mundane, and the generic. The goal of the Übermensch is to reinvent himself in a brave new world where he is the creator of his own being; he is to prove that man is the smith of one's own destiny. Nietzsche didn't prescribe specifics, no exact path one must follow, or a set of rules one must conform to; that is for the prophets. Instead, he insisted that the modern man must rise above his pitfalls and realize his full potential, and make the most of the time given to him on this earth, firmly grounded with his full focus on this life rather than the uncertain beyond or imaginary universes. Perfection for such a creature is the final goal.

How should we define perfection for man of the twenty-first century? True perfection is not a realistic outcome, for we are imperfect creatures living in an imperfect world—after all, we are all too human. That is not to say that one shouldn't strive for perfection. Perfection is to excel, to always give one's best effort, and to push one's own limits. The realization of one's full potential is achieved through determination and hard work. Michelangelo spent three years chiseling the statue of *David*, completed in 1504. Rembrandt similarly devoted three years to the completion of *The Night Watch* in 1642. Victor Hugo began writing *Notre-Dame de Paris* in 1829, which was first published in 1831. Giuseppe Verdi began to conceive *La Traviata* after reading the novel *The Lady of the Camellias* by Alexander Dumas son in 1848; the opera premiered in 1853. These are only but a few examples of great works of art, literature, and music which required great dedication from their creators—a quality quite absent from the modern kidult.

With that in mind, I would like to compare the man of the twenty-first century to this idealist Übermensch, who was conceived at the end of the nineteenth century, to try to extrapolate the progress (or lack thereof) we've made as a whole since. In some form or other we have achieved a sense of strong individualism (in the West at least). The self is free, independent, and exalted. Never before have women possessed as much freedom and respect as men. Minorities are groups of emancipated beings who have achieved equal rights and representation. Society as a whole in the Western world has never been as diverse, with many different nationalities, races, and religious views all living together harmoniously in one giant melting pot (for the most part). Gays and lesbians have earned a great deal of respect and dignity from a crowd who not so long ago condemned them to the pyre, or to the town square to be beaten with rocks until dead. And they rightfully deserve such respect and dignity! Humanity has shed much of its barbarous hide. Society has made a giant leap forward.

In recent times, however, especially in the United States, we have been witnessing this degree of tolerance toward those who are different or who hold different views slowly fading away. One cannot discuss hotly debated topics with loved ones without getting into a fierce argument. There is no more common ground, no prospect for meaningful debate; the faculty of reason has simply vanished—one is either on one extreme or the other. How did this come to be all of a sudden? Were tolerance and progress all a lie that is now slowly crumbling to pieces in the hands of the infantile narcissistic victim? Have we gone too far or not far enough? How do we break the chains of intolerance and engage in genuinely meaningful debate?

Nietzsche would be quite disappointed were he alive in the here and now to witness humanity devolved into lazy unreasonable adults who seek to spoil the very heavens with their insolence and destroy what has been built before their time and before their miserable existence. He created the image of a being who would forge a new world from a blank slate, detached from past mistakes and misjudgments, to start anew. Instead, we look at the past and we're overcome by anger and lust for vengeance. It is high time that we forgave our ancestors and looked ahead, to a brighter future where everyone could be happy and content, or at least tried to be.

How could one be truly happy when one is in a state of constant internal conflict? Our instincts demand satisfaction while our conscious demands discomfort. It is a never-ending swirling vortex of feelings, demands, and obligations. All we can truly do is strive for a balance

where too little is adequate and too much is not insuffi-
cient.

The Green Frenzy

*Thank God men cannot fly, and lay waste the sky
as well as the earth.*

—Henry David Thoreau

N ow that we've briefly identified the Beast, analyzed its qualities, and quantified its habits, it's
time we observed its hunting grounds. You may
recall that in 2018, a teenage girl by the name of Greta
Thunberg became a global sensation. She is a fierce activist for action against climate change. She criticizes
world leaders for their failure to act to protect mother
nature; she attends high-profile conferences and incites
school strikes around the world, and this shining career
of hers began when she was only a high school student.
It is admirable that a fifteen-year-old (at the time she began her environmental activism) is so outspoken and involved in the climate change discourse. However, in the
process of inserting herself as a martyr to shame politicians, she is setting an example for children across the
world, whether it be for good or bad.

Activism among adolescents has become increasingly
widespread. In March 2019, more than a million and a half

young people walked out of schools all over the world in protests against inaction by politicians to tackle climate change.[30] Children are naturally irrational beings. What better orators could there be to address the growing masses of infantile adults than their own children? The child has long been the obsession of the aging adult, and to celebrate that fact, we have placed our idol as the very crown jewel to represent the dire need to address the extremely complicated and delicate phenomenon of climate change. I'm not in any way attempting to discredit climate change. On the contrary—I agree with the message, but I do not trust the messengers' credibility and consequently that the message is making an actual impact.

Yes, we are polluting the planet beyond repair, we are cutting down the Amazon, overfishing the oceans, and running the place into the ground! The echoes of all the wailing cries to act and to preserve nature have made us nothing but blind to the reality and the extent of our recklessness. Tragedies play out in front of our eyes every single day. We are constantly bombarded by carefully worded and just as shocking images of starving children, murders, shootings, and barbarous acts of violence. The media is all too happy to provide those to us in a heinous marketing scheme to capture our attention and keep it.

---

[30] Carrington, Damian. "School Climate Strikes: 1.4 Million People Took Part, Say Campaigners." *The Guardian*. 03/19/2019. https://www.theguardian.com/environment/2019/mar/19/school-climate-strikes-more-than-1-million-took-part-say-campaigners-greta-thunberg. Accessed 05/17/2022.

Tragedy has become banal and unmoving to the crowds of information consumers; it is merely a swipe away from being buried and forgotten until the next day when the scenes play out again, competing for our undivided and desensitized attention.[31]

Did it not occur to anyone that there is so much pollution not only because of the amount of garbage we produce but because this blue marble is overpopulated? It seems logical and common sense that everyone should know this fact, but nobody cares to ever mention it. Nobody at a climate protest has ever said, "Stop overpopulating the planet!" The current total world population stands at 7.872 billion, the majority of which live in China (1.407 billion) and India (1.390 billion), which together account for 35 percent of the global population. The USA stands at 331 million, and the EU is at 447 million. At number four is Indonesia, with 275 million, and at number five is Pakistan with 238 million.[32] If we now refer to the estimated amount of CO_2 emissions for the year 2020, the math looks familiar: China expelled 10.67 billion metric tons (mt) of CO_2 into the atmosphere, India 2.44 billion mt, the United States 4.71 billion mt, the EU 2.6 billion mt. There was a total of 34.81 billion mt of CO_2, which awards

---

[31] Bruckner, Pascal. *The Temptation of Innocence: Living in the Age of Entitlement.* Algora Publishing. 2000. pp. 258-261.
[32] United States Census Bureau. "US and World Population Clock." 2022. https://www.census.gov/popclock/world. Accessed 01/25/2022.

China a 31 percent share, India 7 percent, the USA 14 percent, and the EU 7 percent.[33] In fact, China, India, and the rest of Asia released 20.32 billion mt, or a whopping 58 percent of global CO_2 emissions. The biggest contributor to air pollution is none other than China, the workshop of the West. Long gone are the days when Britain was the workshop of the world, the same title then belonging to Germany in the twentieth century, and now in the hands of China only within the last forty years or so. Bloomberg reported that in 2019, China was responsible for the same amount of CO_2 as the next four countries combined.[34] It is practically suicide to walk outdoors in a large Chinese city without a mask to stop the particulate matter from poisoning your lungs. It is a vicious cycle—burn coal to generate electricity, use that electricity to run air conditioning units to survive the smog, then burn more coal, and so on.

It seems to me that Greta Thunberg has been preaching to the wrong choir, commendable as it is. All countries need to do more, but China is the place she should direct her anger. It is estimated that by 2060, we will have reached a milestone—10 billion people.[35] By the end of

[33] Our World in Data. "CO2 Emissions." 2022. https://ourworldindata.org/co2-emissions. Accessed 01/25/2022.
[34] Wu, Jin. Kan, Karoline. "The Chinese Companies Polluting the World More Than Entire Nations." *Bloomberg News*. 10/24/2021. https://www.bloomberg.com/graphics/2021-china-climate-change-biggest-carbon-polluters/. Accessed 01/25/2022.
[35] WorldOMeter.com. "World Population Milestones." 2022. http://srv1.worldometers.info/world-population/. Accessed 01/25/2022.

the century, there will be 10.8 billion people on the planet. We clearly cannot allow the world population to continue ballooning if we are to tackle climate change.

If we look at the chart titled World Population by Region,[36] we see that three regions have a fertility rate greater than 2.0—Africa (4.4), Oceania (2.4), and Asia (2.2). Compare Africa's 4.4 to Europe's 1.6, Northern America's 1.8, and Latin America's and the Caribbean's 2.0. All regions of the globe except Africa have very similar fertility rates. There are many socio-economic reasons for this, but what we should focus our attention on is the impact this high fertility rate is having. Take this for instance: Kenyans and charities were moved by a widow, Ms. Kitsao, who was cooking stones for her children.[37] Ms. Kitsao has had no work washing laundry since the Coronavirus pandemic began, and she cannot read and write. She has eight children whom she hoped would fall asleep while she pretended to be cooking. She has since received monetary donations to keep her family comfortable and fed. Nobody should bear the burden of not being able to feed their children; no child should ever be starved! As shocking and heartbreaking as this story is, I cannot help but wonder how people who live in poverty all their lives manage to feed eight children on any given day. A lot of people will disagree when I say this, but I

---

[36] Ibid.

[37] BBC.com. "Coronavirus: Kenyans Moved by Widow Cooking Stones for Children." 04/30/2020. https://www.bbc.com/news/world-africa-52494404. Accessed. 01/25/2022.

think it is cruel to the children to have them and not be able to feed them. The parents of such families may not realize it, but put yourselves in the children's shoes!

There are hundreds of charities out there whose sole purpose is to help Africans but very few that I've heard of that work to empower Western families to adopt African children in need. Very little publicity is given to the endeavor. Africa is home to fifty-three million orphans, which accounts for 37 percent of all orphans in the world.[38] Perhaps a stronger focus on adoption would do more good for African orphans than sending them bags of wheat. There are plenty of gay couples in rich countries who want to adopt children in need and provide them with a good start for decent lives! More importantly, however, people in African countries need better health care, coupled with affordable contraceptives. After all, wouldn't one be more conscientious in the creation of dependent human beings if one had a condom handy, given that one cannot afford to feed more mouths?

While we're on the topic of the out-of-control fertility rate of Africa, let us also not forget that China has been pouring billions of dollars into Africa, through its Belt and Road initiative, for infrastructure. Infrastructure brings with it better food supply and healthcare, which

---

[38] Struble, Keegan. "10 Facts About Orphans in Africa." The Borgen Project. 2018. https://borgenproject.org/10-facts-orphans-in-africa/ Accessed 2/27/2022

in turn will, to some extent, allow for the sustainability of the high fertility rate and significantly reduce famine. China helps Africa tackle hunger through investments instead of bags of wheat. Imagine if and when the African continent explodes industrially as Asia has in the last century, using fossil fuels to power its economy: What chance do we stand at keeping the 1.5°C promise?

Tragedy after tragedy is displayed in front of us, and we simply sit calmly and unabashed, drained mentally and physically by the pendulum of grief, reveling in the misery which grips the entire planet. Another such tragic scene has played out in the world which demands our unquestioned compassion and dedication to the global environmental activist movement. Due to the intense heat wave which gripped British Columbia in June of 2021, a heat stroke patient was admitted to the emergency room.[39] The attending doctor wrote down that the underlying reason for the patient's hospitalization was *climate change*. According to the physician's testimony, the case was so severe that he allowed himself to include climate change as a cause of her ailment. The same physician, along with other colleagues, started the Doctors and Nurses for Planetary Health group to advocate for

---

[39] Eveleth, Rose. "Your Medical History Might Someday Include 'Climate Change.'" WIRED. 01/18/2022. https://www.wired.com/story/climate-change-health-medicine/. Accessed 01/25/2022.

better health by protecting the environment.[40] Indeed the situation is so dire that even doctors are taking notice and action. The climate of the world has changed in the last twenty years: springs are short to non-existent, summers are hotter, winters are harsher, floods are more frequent and severe, and wildfires are also. Would I go as far as to insert climate change as a cause for a specific condition? However, who am I to judge? In another twenty years in medical literature, climate change may be to heat stroke as obesity is to heart failure today, as ironic as it may sound.

---

[40] Thompson, Michelle. "Doctor Blames Asthma Suffered by Patient on 'Climate Change' after Historic Heat Wave Killed 500 in Canada." The Daily Mail. 11/07/2021. https://www.dailymail.co.uk/news/article-10175735/A-Canadian-doctor-diagnosed-patient-climate-change-saying-health-problems-worsened.html. Accessed 01/29/2022.

Electric Messianism

We should, and eventually will, have no other choice but to move away from the use of fossil fuels. It may not be immediately and completely possible, but the less we are reliant on them, the better for us and Mother Nature. However, what the environmental gurus refuse to accept is that the transition cannot take place so swiftly. Hydroelectric power is reliable (outside of drought season) and has been around for a long time, yet it is not enough to replace energy generation methods powered by fossil fuels. Nuclear energy is frowned upon by the apocalyptic environmentalist. The European Union seems to be on the right track to classifying nuclear as green energy, yet the angry, misguided environmentalists' concerns must be heard and debated, lest their voices are drowned in the cacophony of doom. So what is left? Solar and windmill farms. Firstly, the sun doesn't shine twenty-four hours a day, nor does the wind blow as much. Also, sun rays and wind are not evenly distributed across the globe. Moreover, because of their intermittent nature and uneven geographical distribution, solar and wind farms (and residential installations) must store power inside batteries. Our current battery technology (Li-ion) is far from environmentally friendly—lithium is difficult and costly to extract from lithium petalite, and the process releases a great amount of pollution. Lithium mining is so damaging to the environment that a recent European mining project in Montalegre, Portugal, was canceled because of the local population's environmental concerns.[41]

Technological evolution, undoubtedly, has a major role to play in solving our earthly existential dilemmas. There are quite a few contenders for the future of energy generation and storage: hydrogen fuel, solid-state batteries, redox flow batteries, and others. However, until such new technologies start turning from prototypes into mass-produced products, we have to live with Li-ion batteries whose useful life ranges anywhere from two thousand to ten thousand charging cycles, depending on manufacturer, quality, and application. Li-ion is currently the most practical energy storage component available to the public in virtually any electrical application—smart devices, computers, solar and wind systems, and electric vehicles.

Electric vehicles (EVs) are to be saviors of mankind and a multitude of other species on Earth. They have been available for a decade or two now to the consumer, but why is it that EVs have not gained as much momentum as one so concerned with global warming would expect? Electric vehicles are great on paper but suffer serious drawbacks, just as internal combustion engine (ICE) vehicles. Realistically, most people don't keep a vehicle

---

[41] Hernández-Morales, Aitor. Diogo, Sofia. "Portugal to Scrap Lithium Mining Project." Politico. 04/27/2021. https://www.politico.eu/article/portugal-lithium-mining-project-scrap/. Accessed 01/25/2022.

for more than ten years in the USA, which increased to twelve years due to the price hikes for used vehicles during the Coronavirus pandemic.[42] For one, switching to all electric won't solve the problem of traffic congestion. Also, it costs money to charge an electric vehicle; it may not be much in dollar amounts, but if everyone were to acquire an EV and plug it in overnight, the power grid would simply collapse. There is also the issue of battery degradation, which varies wildly by manufacturer and model. As a rule of thumb, don't expect to buy an EV whose battery will last you twenty years before it needs replacement. In 2019 the average cost of battery pack replacement was $176/kWh[43] before labor, taxes, fees, etc. It is estimated that battery pack costs will drop to $120–$135/kWh by 2025, and to $62/kWh in 2030. Given the urgency to address greenhouse emissions, these numbers are not as impressive as they should be, and estimates are not guaranteed.

Another serious issue in the electrification of mobility for all Americans (and earthlings in general) is the fact that to upgrade and enhance the power grid, utility companies are going to raise electricity rates to pay for those

[42] Colias, Mike. "Americans Are Keeping Their Cars Longer, as Vehicle Age Hits 12 Years." *The Wall Street Journal*. 2021. https://www.wsj.com/articles/average-u-s-vehicle-age-hits-record-12-years-11623680640. Accessed 01/25/2022.

[43] Lutsey, Nic and Nicholas, Michael. "Update in Electric Vehicle Costs in the United States Through 2030." International Council On Clean Transportation. 2019. https://theicct.org/sites/default/files/publications/EV_cost_2020_2030_20190401.pdf. Accessed 02/09/2022.

upgrades. They won't just pay for it with their profits simply out of the goodness of their hearts. If the Federal and/or local governments are to subsidize the purchase and installation of public EV charging stations, for instance, that money ultimately will come out of the taxpayer's pocket.

A more serious issue with EVs that I'd like to draw attention to is their current price related to range. To get an EV-equivalent of an ICE entry-level automobile in the $25,000–$30,000 price range and a three hundred-plus-mile range will cost you upward of $35,000,[44] which is the starting price of a luxury vehicle. As an average consumer, why would anyone pay for something with inferior features, interior, and mile range when one could buy an ICE German-made luxury car for the same amount of money? The average income of households who owned an EV from 2010 through 2014 was $140,448,[45] which was substantially higher than the average household income of $117,795 for the same period. This statistic, on its own and without accounting for inflation since 2014, suggests that average- and lower-income families simply cannot afford one. Affordability is the main problem that EV manufacturers must solve for all of humanity.

[44] Romans, Brent. "Cheapest Electric Cars." Edmunds.com Inc. 11/24/2022. https://www.edmunds.com/electric-car/articles/cheapest-electric-cars/. Accessed 02/09/2022.
[45] Xing, Jianwei; Leard, Benjamin and Li, Shanjun. "What Does an Electric Vehicle Replace?" National Bureau of Economic Research. 2019. Revised 2021. https://www.nber.org/papers/w25771. Accessed 02/09/2022.

Affordability is also the barring gate to other environmentally friendly initiatives. I, for instance, truly want to go completely green and off the grid; there are plenty of benefits for that, and not just for the environment, but for one's own pocket as well. An installation of a residential solar panel array acts not only as a safeguard against power outages but can also, depending on location and time of year, dramatically reduce one's electric bill and carbon footprint. It unfortunately remains only a dream for far too many Americans. To cover one's roof with solar panels, on average, costs between $10,626 and $13,230 after the 30 percent federal solar tax credit,[46] more than double the cost to replace the entire roof ($4,707–$10,460).[47]

The wake-up call to move away from fossil fuels has been falling on deaf ears for decades and may, unfortunately, be too late to prevent the infamous 1.5°C of global temperature increase. More people should have taken notice thirty years ago when solar-powered water heaters were popping up on roofs in neighborhoods across Europe. Utility companies should have the majority of the grid powered by renewable sources by now, nuclear

---

[46] HomeGuide. "How Much Do Solar Panels Cost?" HomeGuide. 2022. https://homeguide.com/costs/solar-panel-cost. Accessed 05/22/2022.
[47] HomeGuide. "How Much Does A New Roof Replacement Cost?" HomeGuide. 2022. https://homeguide.com/costs/roof-replacement-cost. Accessed 05/22/2022.

included, but they don't[48] because investing in green energy isn't making their shareholders a profit in the near term, and the long term is too long to wait for a return on investment. The US federal and local governments should not be looking to dismantle perfectly operational nuclear power plants and in the process make electricity unaffordable for a large number of citizens, because solar and wind cannot fully replace nuclear. Instead, our politicians should accept the fact that, despite numerous concerns, the process of nuclear fission produces zero greenhouse emissions. The prophecy of the green messianism will not come to pass while the West continues to produce most of its consumer products in a China largely powered by coal. Multibillionaires will not pave the way for humanity's electrified mobility. They will and already are paving it for those with already deep enough pockets. Multibillionaires will also not colonize space for everyone but only for a select few who will have the money to buy a ticket when this planet becomes uninhabitable due to our own stupidity.

The global warming debate can go on for decades. We can complain and yell and bicker about it. We can all become fierce activists and bang on the doors of governments and politicians and make outlandish demands, but change will not happen as swiftly as we want it to, not

---

[48] US Energy Information Administration. "US Energy Facts Explained." 2022. https://www.eia.gov/energyexplained/us-energy-facts/. Accessed 06/05/2022.

unless the change starts with us. Every single person who cares about the environment needs to put those words to action and show true responsibility, one worthy of adulthood. Take short showers, recycle everything you can, turn the lights off when you exit a room, and buy energy-efficient appliances. We've been hearing those suggestions for years, but here's one more in line with the trends of today: stop using streaming services. Cloud computing accounts for 4 percent of global greenhouse gas emissions and is estimated to double by 2025.[49]

[49] Griffiths, Sarah. *Why your internet habits are not as clean as you think. Smart Guide to Climate Change.* BBC.com. https://www.bbc.com/future/article/20200305-why-your-internet-habits-are-not-as-clean-as-you-think Accessed 02/03/2022

Plastic Culture

Are you one of those people who are tired of every food item at the grocery store being sold in non-recyclable plastic wrapping and boxes? Does that compel you to email your representative? Don't email your representative. Instead, email the company that made the product and tell them how you feel about all the plastic waste their company contributes to. Find alternatives to plastic and commit to reducing your environmental footprint. It's easy to complain and demand change, but change begins from within, not from without.

Think about the damage plastic has done to the earth, the oceans, marine life, and us. Think about all of the disposable face masks we've dumped into the environment in the last two years since the COVID-19 turmoil began! The streets were, and many around the world still are, littered with them. Countless nasty masks were and are floating in rivers, lakes, and oceans. The World Health Organization itself felt compelled to bring to our attention to what a poor job we've done with the proper disposal and recycling of face masks, COVID tests, and vaccine waste. Most of the eighty-seven thousand tons of personal protective equipment shipped around the world through a joint UN emergency initiative has ended up in either landfills, rivers, or oceans.[50] Everybody was so scared of contracting COVID-19 that they completely forgot about the environment. Plastic takes more than one human life to fully degrade, and not truly degrade. In the process, it turns into microscopic particles that pollute everything. Fish eat those little pieces of plastic, and other marine life ends up as the victims of plastic bags, strangled and washed ashore with passers-by paying no attention to the atrocities but only to their fitness watches, telling them to jog another five feet and to drink a glass of water. According to a recent WWF report, 88 percent of all marine species that it studied are severely affected by plastic contamination.[51] This is the heritage that our plastic culture is leaving for the generations after us—islands of plastic garbage floating around the oceans! There is not a single pristine place on this Earth that man has not touched and spoiled with his insolence and self-importance.

The state of California has launched an extensive investigation into an alleged conspiracy played by the oil and petrochemical industries.[52] The state alleges that the

[50] World Health Organization. Global analysis of healthcare waste in the context of COVID-19: status, impacts, and recommendations. 02/01/2022. p. 9. https://www.who.int/publications/i/item/9789240039612. Accessed 02/01/2022.
[51] Deutsche Welle. "Plastic Pollution in Oceans Growing Dramatically, WWF Warns." https://p.dw.com/p/46etL. Accessed 02/07/2022.
[52] Rust, Susanne. Xia, Rosanna. "State Accuses Exxon Mobil of Deceiving Public, Perpetuating 'Myth' of Plastics Recycling." *Los Angeles Times.*

aforementioned industries willfully deceived the public about the recyclability of plastics. We are to believe that it is solely the fossil fuel industries' fault for the irreversible and utter trashing of our planet. It is as if the fossil fuel companies forced every one of us to produce everything with plastic, wrap everything in plastic, and create piles and piles of plastic, enough to bury Mount Everest beneath all this plastic. Plastic is everywhere, in every little nook, cranny, and corner of the world, but it isn't solely the extractor's fault. It isn't solely the manufacturer's fault. It is you, my fellow citizen, who is to blame also for all this plastic garbage. The *Übermenschen* of today's day and age don't care if everything he or she (or it, for that matter) consumes is made of plastic and that all this plastic will end up in a landfill and/or in rivers, oceans, and even in the rain. All that His and Her Highnesses the baby lords care about is convenience. Single-use ("disposable") plastic diapers are convenient, plastic water bottles are convenient, zipper plastic bags are convenient, plastic cups and utensils are convenient, plastic food packaging is convenient, and plastic toothbrushes and plastic floss picks are as well. Plastic-made "necessities" are not only convenient but also cheap and easy to toss away, and hence the mindless self-absorbed whiners

---

04/28/2022. https://www.latimes.com/environment/story/2022-04-28/california-blames-exxonmobil-for-plastic-pollution-crisis. Accessed 05/02/2022.

are happy, but when they are confronted with the consequences of their actions, they are never to blame. It is always someone else's fault! However, an old saying states: "That which you do onto yourself even God couldn't do to you."

At the bottom of our plastic culture is hypocrisy, hypocrisy which is rampant and omnipresent, and everybody is guilty of it: from every politician to every businessman to every little innocent crybaby citizen in every country in this plastic wasteland of a planet. Keep staring at those smartwatches; one day soon they may caution you to watch your water, or you may gag on a piece of plastic or two!

The Wheel of Fate

Every man is guilty of all the good he did not do.

—Voltaire

The United States, Europe, and the West have been under relentless attack for a few decades now. Enemies abound—from without and from within. Have we forgotten al-Qaeda, ISIL/ISIS/IS, and other bands of barbarians, jihadists, and live kamikazes who believe that nine virgins will be waiting for them in heaven as a reward for murdering innocent Westerners? Have we been so quick to brush aside the horrors of September 11, the 2004 Madrid train bombings, the 2005 London Underground bombings, and the 2015 Paris attacks, or are the reactions to the 2020 riots any indication that we have become indifferent to the labors of terrorism?

Europe has, since WWII, taken a pacifist approach to existence, determined at all costs to prevent more wars on the continent. Putin and his lackeys are now seeking to exploit this approach and decimate Ukraine and its people and retake his "motherlands." Thankfully, his miscalculations are having a backfire effect. Europe, the West, and its allies have drawn the line and reassessed the number of determined enemies they have attracted after having been preoccupied with climate change phantasms.

Anti-Americanism, and Anti-Westernism in general, have morphed beyond the murdering of civilians in the name of whatever perverted vision of justice one wishes to invoke, or acts of war against Western and West-friendly peoples. The 1619 project, where journalists and their employers, proclaiming themselves as competent historians, seek to desecrate our heritage with the claim that the American Revolution was conducted to preserve slavery.[53] It has drawn sharp criticism from historians holding proper credentials giving them the authority to evaluate historical facts, but still, its legacy endures and seeks to infuse further hate within the population. It isn't the only project determined to rewrite history and portray the White Man as the "American cowboy"[54] and the prime evil on Earth. Multicultural historians have been busy replacing Western civilization academic courses with more "truthful" world history teachings, placing emphasis on connections rather than empirical evidence.[55]

[53] Warren Jr, Jack. *The Fatal Flaw of the 1619 Project Curriculum.* The American Revolution Institute of the Society of the Cincinnati. 08/14/2020. https://www.americanrevolutioninstitute.org/fatal-flaw-of-the-1619-project-curriculum/. Accessed 06/13/2022.
[54] CNN. "Attacks Draw Mixed Response in Mideast." 09/12/2001. https://web.archive.org/web/20071101150055/http://archives.cnn.com/2001/WORLD/europe/09/12/mideast.reaction/index.html Accessed. 06/13/2022.
[55] Duchesne, Ricardo. *Faustian Man in a Multicultural Age.* Arktos Media Ltd. 2017. pp. 99-100.

Has anyone bothered to notice how it has become politically incorrect to be white in a world that white man
built? It almost seems like it happened overnight. It is
"out of fashion" to be white, and a man on top of that—
be it straight or gay. It's all the same to today's anti-
Americanists, calling themselves "progressive" activists
(quotations here are appropriate because liberalism, or
progressivism, totally rejects any forms of extremism
which may derive from it).

Exaggerated as the above statement may sound, it
isn't too far from reality in the United States. Ever since
the demise of colonialism, the man of European origin
has done nothing but languish himself for past mistakes,
including imperialism, slavery, and exploitation of others
and the environment. This guilt-driven self-sadism has
been entrenched into our psyche, and the White Man has
simply become irrelevant in his own home.

Combine this lethargy and sense of guilt with the unrelenting attacks on our values, both physical and psychological, and you have a textbook recipe for the decadence of our Western world. Cultural Marxism is seeking
to transform our Western culture by introducing politically correct morals and "minority supremacy"[56] as vehicles to demonize any discussions of white pride and
white identity. Critical race theorists and their accomplices, as we'll discover later in the next two chapters, are
targeting our legal and monetary systems to rid them of

---

[56] Ibid. pp. 27-28.

systemic racism and inequitable treatment. The rise of communist China as an economic and military world power, through their Belt and Road initiative, is threatening not only further adoption of Western principles across the world but also the very fabric of the West. Some have declared that our civilization is already in a state of decay. Others are sounding the alarm that it may be looming over the horizon. Whatever the case may be, one cannot simply forsake thousands of years of the delicate and complex evolution of our Western civilization to be replaced by Marxist and communist utopias, which we fought tooth and nail not too long ago. Liberty, justice, and the pursuit of happiness are engrained in our constitution and are causes worth defending in the face of relentless ideological rivals.

European Legacy

In an attempt to defend the legacy of the White Man, we must examine and call out the positive aspects of our society that make it Western, or dare I say European! This method shall allow us to better understand these foundational pillars and ascertain the tremendous value they bring to our Western world, compared to other countries gripped by authoritarian regimes, lack of human and civil rights, economic misery, and lawlessness.

The Western world, the legacy of White Man, is a broad term that we must define before further exploration. In essence, the West represents parts of the globe where all the following are applied: a democratic system of governing, equal civil rights and liberties for all, a high degree of industrialization, a developed free market, and Greco-Roman values.[57] All of these characteristics trace their origins to the European continent—democracy, humanism, rationalism, industry, and capitalism. Those are the very foundations of our civilization, which we must cherish and protect.

---

[57] Ibid. p. 10. For Prof. Duchesne there are additional critical aspects of the West to be called the West: Christianity, Indo-European languages and European culture. He abstains from including Eastern Europe, Russia, Japan, India, South Korea and Latin America from his definition of the West as these regions of the globe either lack European culture or are lagging behind on democratic values.

Firstly, the *democratic* form of government, which is at the heart of our governmental institutions, originated in Athens in the early sixth century BC. Decision-making in public affairs was exercised directly by the citizens themselves through the most powerful body of government, the assembly,[58] an early incarnation of parliament or senate. Aristotle (384–322 BCE) defined democracy as a "right" constitution that is directed to the common interest of all citizens and in which the people are sovereign (as opposed to "perverted" forms of government which were aimed at the selfish interest of the ruling body).[59] Democracy declares the poor and the rich on an equal level. The state's existence is to provide "the good life," for the people, by the people.

Modern democracy has learned to incorporate another important principle into its essence—the autonomy of the *individual*. The people maintain sovereignty, but their power must be limited to the borders of an individual's personal life.[60] Personal fulfillment is a perfectly worthy cause for the existence of the individual—the message that *humanism* has sought to promote through the ages. Since antiquity, humanists have championed the ideal that human beings possess free will and therefore are entitled to personal freedom, autonomy, and well-being. Kant argued that it is by the propagation of

[58] Aristotle. *Politics*. 1297a14.
[59] Ibid. 1278b6.
[60] Todorov, Tzvetan. *The Inner Enemies of Democracy*. English Edition. Polity Press. 2014. p. 8.

the arts and sciences that humanists have given the individual agency, have civilized him, and to some extent
have contributed to his morality.[61] The humanities have
brought pleasure and refinement to society in which all
men and women take the reins of their own destinies and
lead a good life:[62] literature, fine art, history, and philosophy allow the self to enrich the soul and transcend the
common, banal, and simple. As Petrarch (1304–1374), who
may be called the first humanist, phrased it, "It is better
to will the good than to know the truth."

The fusion of democracy and humanism (individualism) is the pinnacle of modern society: the community
should not interfere with the personal lives of individuals,
and in turn, the individual must not impose their own interests on the people. Enlightenment thinkers such as
Montesquieu and Rousseau realized that humanism has
its limits—the individual's will has the power to improve
his life, but it cannot spill into despotism by imposing
one's will on others; everything must be held in moderation, and a balance of powers must be maintained.

Secondly, an indispensable principle to European and
Western thought is that of *rationalism*, or the ability of an
individual to employ *reason*. The examination of the faculty of reason spans centuries back to Plato (c.427–c.347

---

[61] Kant, Immanuel. *Critique of Judgement*. Oxford University Press. 2008. p.
262.
[62] The definition of *the good life* now looks to occupy a second dimension. It
is to be applied not only in the context of the community but in the personal fulfillment of every living soul.

BCE) and his apprentice Aristotle. For an individual to exhibit reason, he must apply logic based on new or existing conclusions in the pursuit of truth. There are three means by which an individual can achieve goodness and virtuousness: nature, habit, and reason.[63]. While all animate beings rely on the guidance of natural impulse, or instincts, humans are the only ones capable of employing reason in order to follow a better course of action than what instinct or habit drives them to do.[64] So important is this human skill of reason that Aristotle concluded that the function of a good man is to lead a life in accordance with the rational principle; human goodness is contained in activities of soul-establishing virtues.[65]

So far we've demonstrated that European philosophers have laid the foundations for a society where the individual's purpose is to live a good life by engaging in virtuous activities guided by reason, in a state ruled by all individuals. For the people of a given state to lead a good life, they must engage in the production of goods and services and commerce. Charles-Louis de Secondat, Baron de Montesquieu (1689–1755), is credited as the champion of constitutional government as we know it in the United States today: a government where the principle of separation of powers rules supreme.[66] He argued

---

[63] Aristotle. *Politics*. 1332a38.
[64] Ibid. 1332b2.
[65] Aristotle. *The Nicomachean Ethics*. 1098a10-1098a15.
[66] Bailey, Andrew et al. *The Broadview Anthology of Social and Political Thought*. Vol I. Broadview Press. 2008. p. 577.

that a despotic state benefits no one, including the despot. He asserted that the most likely method to ensure
liberty and repel suppression was to split the government
into executive, legislative, and judicial branches. Montesquieu's image of the individual at the time shined with the
spirit of commerce. For citizenry to enjoy a high degree
of freedom, their countries must excel at trade, as witnessed by England and Holland in the eighteenth century. Constitutional government and commerce are in-
separable, and his vision was highly influential in the
founding of our great country.[67]

Lastly, we must delve into the economic forces which
shape our time. From the late eighteenth through the
middle of the nineteenth centuries, a period known as the
Industrial Revolution, the spirit of trade would conquer
the world. The vast amount of capital amassed in Great
Britain, Continental Europe, and the United States during the age of mercantilism enabled investments in machinery for the purpose of mass production. The increase
in supply created strong demand for basic commodities
due to the redistribution of labor, in turn ensuring a mass
consumer market. Adam Smith's (1723–1790) *The Wealth of
Nations* (1776) was instrumental in the development of
modern-day *capitalism*. He asserted that the prudential
self-interest of the individual provided the primary psychological drive for economic relationships. Markets
should be free of political interference so that the pursuit

---

[67] Ibid. p. 578.

of every person's own good could ensure the promotion of the collective outcome.[68] Smith's analysis of the division of labor laid the groundwork for a boom in manufacturing. His arguments for free trade within nations and among them led to the evolution of capitalist economies into the present day.

To conclude our brief overview of Western foundations, it was European thinkers who developed the pillars of what we call a Western society: individualism and rationalism coupled with the democratic form of governing and the capitalistic economic system. The United States was built in the European image, but it isn't a faithful copy. It took the best traits and sought to improve the worst. European settlers carried with them the flame in their hearts that is as essential to the foundations of a free country as mortar is to brick—the Faustian spirit. It is the soul who sees deeds done as more important than mere existence in the fight for survival; it is the soul who traverses the furthest parts of the world and reaches ever higher into the heavens; it is the soul who conquers the world and shapes it, who embodies an aristocrat, a hero, a legend. What sets the United States apart from its European origins is freedom. The pinnacle of civilization, the living dream that is America, is not capitalism or democracy per se, but freedom, which guarantees that capitalism and democracy flourish. Our founding fathers

---

[68] Ibid. pp. 719-720.

broke the clutches of British tyranny and fulfilled the destiny of the New World: *liberty* and pursuit of happiness through self-governance. What is this sort of liberty that only the American experiment offers? It is liberty, which is power and responsibility, wisdom and humility, thrill and ambition, a goal, an inspiration, a purpose.

Attack on White Heritage

The West is White Man's legacy to the world, and the very fabric of the West is under attack not just from outside but also from within. The crown jewels of our society are liberty, justice, and the pursuit of happiness. Liberty implies civil liberties and equal rights; by justice, we mean equality before the eyes of the law; the pursuit of happiness simply entails that everyone has the ability to live their lives as they see fit (so long as they harm no one, if I may add). These three fundamental principles are the reason why our society is so great, so sophisticated, and the envy of the rest of the world. We have centuries of trial and error behind us which have shaped the current state that we live in.

The critics among us would see the White Man surrender complete control of our world to minorities: they argue that White Man is responsible for the suffering colonialism caused, as well as slavery, discrimination, mistreatment, world wars, etc. Therefore the White Man is to live in guilt and shame, forever to burn in the fires of hell for generations to come.

Colonialism, as unfair to numerous local communities as it was, was a key factor in the distribution of our values, our faith, our competitive endeavors, industrialization, a significant increase in the quality of life, and even in some cases, an increase in IQ.[69]

It is thanks to us, people of European descent, that slavery was completely outlawed around the world; European Liberalism led to the abolition of slavery, serfdom, and other injustices upon the individual to the extent of what they call Rights of Man[70] in Europe; we call those civil liberties in the United States. Let us remind ourselves that in the United States, the Emancipation Proclamation of 1863 was issued by president Abraham Lincoln, a white man, who freed the slaves and proclaimed them as equal citizens to the white population.

Our work isn't over in the fight for equal rights for all, but the fact of the matter is that such a liberal system is only present in the West, and the West is the only place where progress is allowed to bloom. Yet those who made it so are portrayed as villains; they are to feel ashamed and repent for the sins of past generations, for acts we,

---

[69] Ibid. p. 36. n. 74.
Michael Pogliano. *The Ethics of Racial Preservation: Frank Salter's on Genetic Interests.* Counter-Currents. 2011. https://counter-currents.com/2011/04/the-ethics-of-racial-preservation-frank-salters-on-genetic-interests/ Accessed 03/01/2022. Pogliano assesses that colonization of Africa brought technology, medicine and social organization to the old continent, which in turn increased the local population's productivity, life expectancy, population, and also average IQ levels.
[70] Salvadori, Massimo. *The Rise of Modern Communism: A Brief History of the Communist Movement in the Twentieth Century.* Henry Holt and Company, New York. 1952. p. 1.

the living, did not commit, acts we do not even intend to commit.

Why should I be ashamed of having been born of pale skin? I treat everybody, regardless of race, color, sex, etc., etc., the same way I would want to be treated—with dignity and respect. Those are the virtues instilled in me by my family and the society I grew up in.

Is it only the West and the White Man who are guilty of slavery? Western colonialists made it a booming transatlantic trade, but they did not invent it, nor did they commercialize it and exploit it well into the twentieth century. Allow me to present to you some context and facts about slavery outside the Americas, Africa, and Western Europe that nobody who claims to be an expert on the history of slavery cares to mention.

The Balkan Peninsula in Eastern Europe was for five hundred years under the yoke of the Ottomans. In their vast empire, slavery, and even sexual slavery,[71] was an integral part of society and the economy, which unfortunately persisted as late as 1908.[72] The Ottoman army had a special class of soldiers called the Janissaries. Those soldiers were none other than young Christian boys taken by force from their homes and converted to Islam

---

[71] Von Schierbrand, Wolf. "Slaves Sold to the Turk; How the Vile Traffic Is Still Carried on in the East." *The New York Times*. 03/28/1886. https://timesmachine.ny-times.com/timesmachine/1886/03/28/106300694.pdf. Accessed 05/21/2022.
[72] Dursteler, Eric. *Venetians in Constantinople: Nation, Identity, and Coexistence in the Early Modern Mediterranean.* JHU Press. 2006. p. 72.

by the means of what was called "blood tax," which was imposed upon the local Slavic and Greek communities. This was standard practice in the Balkans.[73]

During the Greek War of Independence that shattered the Ottoman grip on the country, in March of 1822, a revolt took place on the island of Chios. As a result, the forty thousand Turkish troops that arrived were ordered to kill all infants under the age of three, all males twelve years and older, and all females forty and over, except those who were willing to convert to Islam. The town was burned to the ground, and it is estimated that only two thousand people remained on the island, twenty-one thousand managed to escape, fifty-two thousand were massacred, and fifty-two thousand were enslaved.[74] So gruesome was the event that took place on Chios that it provoked international outrage and prompted the French painter Eugène Delacroix to create a depiction of the horror, named *Scenes from the Massacre of Chios*.

In 1876, at the beginning of the April Uprising in an attempt to liberate Bulgaria from Ottoman rule, a battle took place in the small village of Batak. Five thousand Bashi-bozuk, irregular soldiers of the Ottoman army, many of whom were recruited through slavery, surrounded the village. The leader of the Bashi-bozuk, Ahmet Aga, negotiated with the villagers to withdraw his

[73] Anderson, Perry. *Lineages of the Absolutist State*. Verso. 1974. p. 366.
[74] *Revolution – The Massacre of the Island of Chios*. The History of Chios. 2011. https://web.archive.org/web/20111002113325/http://www.chioshistory.gr/en/itx/itx25.html. Accessed 02/10/2022.

troops if the village disarmed. The locals and insurrec-
tionists did so only then to be attacked mercilessly by the
Ottomans.[75] The houses were raided and burned down,
and everyone and everything was shot at. Two hundred
people were hiding in the House of Bogdan; they surren-
dered on the promise to be spared, only to be stripped of
their clothes and belongings in order not to stain them
with blood, and brutally killed—either beheaded, burned
alive, and/or impaled. The mayor of the village, Trendafil
Kerelov, was shot. They gouged his eyes, pulled his teeth
out, impaled him on a stake until it came out through his
mouth, and then roasted him alive, in front of everyone.[76]
The account of Trendafil's son's wife continues the tale:
"At the time this took place, Achmet Aga's son took my
child from my back and cut it to pieces with his sword
before my eyes. Trandafily's charred remains were left ly-
ing there a month, and were then buried."[77]

As you can see, people of the Balkans have much reason to hate Turks, but they've learned to live in peace.
There are considerable minorities of ethnic Turks
throughout the peninsula, and still, even after all the
atrocities that the ancestors of the people of the Balkans
suffered by the ancestors of the Turkish people, there are
no accusations of inherent racism thrown around from

---

[75] More, Robert Jasper. *Under the Balkans. Notes of a Visit to the District of Phil-
ippopolis in 1876.* H. S. King & Co. 1877. p. 86.
[76] Ibid. pp. 105-106.
[77] Ibid. p. 108.

either side. Could we learn something from these Eurasian peoples and how their long and bloody history has shaped their cultures—cultures that have confronted their past and are striving for a better path forward? Does transforming the existence of peoples into the pathos of the Eternal Victim not bring about more misery and suffering? Anti-Americanists disagree.

The constant attempts to reinforce the guilt of past mistakes have taken such a toll that it has gone beyond just a self-destructing mechanism; it has morphed into a means for people of color to exploit this weakness. White people are the only race that exhibits racism; white people are the only ones guilty of discrimination and oppression. No other race is capable of such horrible acts. These are the messages coming out of various Marxist-leaning, anti-Western movements. The wheel has been turning, and now the oppressed peoples of the past are becoming the oppressors of the present. Everybody hates the West, but everybody wants to be here! There was never meant to be a clause in the Diversity Social Contract of the West that minorities will remove White Man from the majority. The Diversity Social Contract is to ensure that minorities will share in the governance of society along with the majority; it never implied that communities of color should exert oppression on the white community.

Every institution, be it public or private, is taking initiatives of diversity representation, meaning at every level, among every board of directors, every employee, actor, news anchor, university professor, and public school teacher, there must be at least one black person, one Latino, one Asian, and so on, regardless of qualifications. Nowadays they are selling this as diversity, but what truly hides behind it is another form of discrimination. A person of color is needed for the position, not another white man! That indeed is the qualifying factor—the color of your skin and damned be meritocracy! If I were to apply for a job and I happened to be perfectly qualified, I may end up not being hired because they needed a purple-skinned Martian to fulfill their diversity inclusion commitment, even if that person was not as qualified as I was. What do you call such a thing if not pure discrimination and racism? This actually is the very definition of racism—some form of prejudice against a person based on race. In essence, this is a classic case of *"Catch the thief!" the thief yelled.*

On the one hand, you have large corporations being sued for gender discrimination over compensation disparities between different groups.[78] On the other, you have "old white guys" retaliating against the same companies for being replaced with a person of color for the

---

[78] Roth, Emma. "Google to Pay $118 Million to Settle Gender Discrimination Lawsuit." *The Verge*. 06/12/2022. https://www.theverge.com/2022/6/12/23164678/google-pay-118-million-settle-gender-discrimination-lawsuit. Accessed 06/13/2022.

sake of equity and inclusion quotas.[79] Has equity and inclusion become a double-edged sword? Are businesses to be locked forever in litigation because there always will be someone unsatisfied with their pay and career advancement opportunities? Previously, we discovered that the Eternal Victim can never be fully satisfied, as the needs of the id are forever endless, always seeking that which they don't possess, but never appreciating what they do have. Could we ever satisfy everyone so that nobody is ever done injustice? Can everyone truly be judged fairly by the same standards, the same scale of performance and worth? Or is it a battle with no end in sight, as the Eternal Victim could never be happy, hiding beneath the mask of equity and inclusion?

The blatant prejudice against white people, masquerading as diversity, is invading all aspects of public and private life, even the language we speak, because we must remove the *white-ness* and *man-ness* from the English language. Such grace, sophistication, and proficiency in the English language, indeed, are exhibited by the use of these two terms! Text processing software's autocorrect feature will suggest politically correct terms when you type, so as not to offend anyone.[80] The lunacy has gone

---

[79] Brooks, Khristopher. "'White Guy' Case Against AT&T Can Move Forward, Judge Says." CBS News. 06/09/2022. https://www.cbsnews.com/news/joseph-dibenedetto-att-race-gender-age-lawsuit-georgia/. Accessed 06/12/2022.
[80] Baker, Sam. "Computer Says No! Showgirl, Mankind, Whitewash, and Blacklist Are Just Some of the Words That Don't Make It Past Microsoft

so far that we must be informed that it is now politically incorrect to use the words postman, mankind, and manpower; instead, we are highly encouraged to substitute them for *mail carrier, humankind,* and *workforce,* respectively, lest somebody takes great offense at being referred to by the highly offensive terms *postman, mankind,* and *manpower.*

White Man has much to be proud of, for all the cultural, economic, social, and civil progress he has brought to this world. It is time White Man shook off the lethargy which he has succumbed to and stood up for himself, in a time when the very fabric of society is under attack by those we protect, elevate, and accept as equal partners. It is time to put the nonsense aside and stand for what is rational.

Word's New Woke Filter (But Don't Worry, You Can Turn It Off)." *Daily Mail.* 2022. https://www.dailymail.co.uk/news/article-10398999/Blacklist-postman-mankind-just-words-wont-fly-Microsofts-woke-filter.html. Accessed 02/20/2022.

The Gathering Storm

Fetter this malefactor to the jagged rocks in adamantine bonds infrangible.

—Aeschylus, *Prometheus Bound*

O ur great country is what it is today thanks to centuries of immigration. We seek the brightest and best from all over the world. That gives us a competitive edge over the rest. Peoples from all races and nationalities join the melting pot, the United States, and become one of us through assimilation. They speak our language(s) and practice our way of life. Then, in turn, their children do so as well, and the children after them.

Over the last few years, ideologies under the vast umbrella of *race theories* have gained great momentum, preaching division, and consequently conflict, between all races in our country. The hottest discussions nowadays revolve around an obscure member of this umbrella called critical race theory (CRT). It claims to only concern itself with the influence of race within the scope of the law and justice system, yet we'll discover that its subject matter and concern are much more subtle than that.

Let us examine the theoretical assumptions that critical race theorists are spreading, and we shall, through critical thinking and a good sense of rationalism, expose its flaws. According to CRT, our society is founded based on the liberal order (rationalism, constitutional law, legal reasoning).[81] We previously observed that our very foundations and principles were created by white people,[82] so their former conclusion aligns with ours. This is where the critical plane of existence splits off from reality. Academic institutions, who have subscribed to the CRT dogma, teach that race is a political and social construct designed to concentrate power specifically with white people and to legitimize this power over non-white people.[83] Critical race theorists then suggest that because race was present in the process of societal and institutional evolution, American social life, political structures, and economic systems are founded upon race or heavily influenced by it. Race has become internalized in the American conscience.[84]

This is quite the leap of faith that logic has had to make. We've gone from *race* being a white invention, to

---

[81] Critical Race Training in Education. "What Is Critical Race Theory?" Legal Insurrection Foundation. 2022. https://criticalrace.org/what-is-critical-race-theory/. Accessed 01/25/2022.

[82] See chapter "The Wheel of Fate," subchapter "European Heritage."

[83] Brandeis University. "Diversity, Equity & Inclusion"—Race. https://www.brandeis.edu/diversity/resources/definitions.html. Accessed 02/05/2022.

[84] Critical Race Training in Education. "What Is Critical Race Theory?" Legal Insurrection Foundation. 2022. https://criticalrace.org/what-is-critical-race-theory/. Accessed 01/25/2022.

race being omnipresent in our institutions, to race defining our very conscience. We have lived with it for centuries, and it has been embroidered within the objective psyche (collective unconscious), which Carl Jung believed to be made up of *archetypes*.[85] The Shadow, as Jung called it, is the unconscious of one's personality where all his evil instincts lie. From there, if we are to believe CRT, our racist selves taunt us with their black visages, and like puppeteers, those apparitions manipulate us in order to maintain the white balance of power.

If we are to be able to identify racism, we must have a way to quantify it. How does one quantify racism? General and racism-specific scales have been created by a union of statisticians and psychologists. One such scale, the Modern Racism Scale[86] seeks to measure what they call *modern racism* through surveys. Modern Racism[87] hypothesizes that racism has evolved into an indirect form from its traditional counterpart. Since there are no remaining laws in the United States of America that objectively display racial prejudice or discrimination against

---

[85] Carl Jung pioneered the idea of the collective unconscious as being a collection of inherited experiences shared by all of humanity.

[86] Morison, Todd and Kiss, Mark. "Modern Racism Scale." Springer International Publishing AG. 2017. https://doi.org/10.1007/978-3-319-28099-8_1251-1. Accessed 02/05/2022.

[87] McConahay, John. "Modern Racism and Modern Discrimination: The Effects of Race, Racial Attitudes, and Context on Simulated Hiring Decisions." *Personality and Social Psychology Bulletin.* 1983. https://journals.sagepub.com/doi/10.1177/0146167283094004. Accessed 02/05/2022.

minorities, racism must have "moved" from the macro-
cosm (laws and regulations) to the microcosm (the individual's subconscious). Even the slightest argument for
reverse discrimination is a manifestation of modern racism.

Modern racism is based on an older concept called
implicit bias, and its right hand, the *implicit association test*,
serves to measure such bias. The premise lies in the unconscious of an individual causing him to do unintended
harm. The skeletal hand stretching from one's subcons-
cience manifests in subtle acts or comments perceived by
minorities, or non-dominant groups, as offensive, and
considered to be micro-aggressions.[88] If we are to listen
to the implicit bias theory, micro-aggressions create systems of oppression. Racism is everywhere, prejudice is
rampant, and we don't even know it! The unconscious,
the Shadow archetype, forces us to commit prejudicial
acts that somebody somewhere will perceive as offensive. We are all guilty, and we must repent!

The scale of power weighs in the favor of whites,
which makes them privileged and prone to white fragility,
another spectacular academic buzzword of the day. CRT
literature defines white fragility as defensive mechanisms
triggered by any fluctuation in the scale where whites are

---

[88] Sue, Derald. *Microaggressions in Everyday Life: Race, Gender, and Sexual Orien-
tation*. Wiley. First Edition. 2010.

deprived of favor or privilege: anger, fear, guilt, argumentation, silence, etc.[89] For white fragility to manifest itself, it requires a white subject. The subject then follows to be prone to exhibit prejudice and discrimination against members of other racial groups, i.e., racism, because those other racial groups would be the ones seeking to even the scales. It is then asserted that it is meaningless to question whether in a given situation racism did happen, but rather one should question the means by which racism manifested.[90] In other words, whenever there is any suspicion or allegation of racism, the validity of such accusation or suspicion mustn't be tested, and it must be assumed that it is valid for all intents and purposes. One is automatically guilty without having to be proven innocent!

Further research into CRT writings shines a light on the nature of racism: it is categorized as descriptive (as opposed to prescriptive), and for racism to be undone, it must be constantly identified, described, and then dismantled.[91] For somebody to be called anti-racist, one must engage in the identification, description, and process of dismantling racism.

---

[89] Brandeis University. "Diversity, Equity & Inclusion"—White Fragility. https://www.brandeis.edu/diversity/resources/definitions.html. Accessed 02/05/2022.
[90] Schroeder, Carole; DiAngelo, Robin. "Addressing Whiteness in Nursing Education." https://robindiangelo.com/wp-content/uploads/2016/01/SchroederDiAngelo-1.pdf p.1. Accessed 02/05/2022.
[91] Kendi, Ibram. *How to Be an Antiracist*. One World Publishing. 2019. p. 9.

Two principles stand out from the previous paragraph:

1. Racism is descriptive. A prescriptive term defines how a given situation *should be*, whereas a descriptive term is one that illustrates what the situation *really is*. For something that *is*, it follows to manifest itself in some form or other. Racism is given life, being, and autonomy. An autonomous entity possesses *will*, the will to interact with reality, exert its influence on it, and cast its web of representations.

2. Racism is to be found and dismembered. Given that racism has acquired a life of its own and has the power to mold reality, then it must be present in our universe (i.e., our psyche, since racism is a psychological phenomenon). If one can discern its manifestations in the individual's psyche, one can and must discover the source in the collective psyche. Once the source is found, it is to be eliminated.

We've so far determined that CRT claims that racism has morphed into a beast on a collective scale where every white person is guilty as charged, and it must be destroyed. How does one dismantle systemic racism? The answer lies in the keyword *equity*. The systematic racism in our institutions has and is leading to different legal, and most importantly, economic outcomes between different racial groups. The definition of the term *equity*, when not relating to company shares or asset value, is (a) "circumstances where everybody is treated equally," and (b) "a system of justice that allows fair judgment where the circumstances aren't covered by existing laws."[92] So equity in common speech does not concern itself with economics, fairness, and outcome within the same meaning, yet CRT-umbrella literature uses it so; a new *prescriptive* (re)definition of the word, of what it *should be.*

The call to action is given, and the objective correlative is defined: all anti-racists, those who are to dismantle systemic racism, are to push for equity and to find racism in their daily lives.[93] They are to see the face of racism everywhere at any time of day, day after day, until all they can see is just that—racism. The *racial* Shadow archetype is turned into a state of collective neurosis. The infidels are to be hunted down and converted, lest they risk being cast out from every aspect of society. A cult obsessed with a single purpose—to unwind the very fabric of society and install a new god, one that will go beyond "colorblindness," one that will deliver them from their suffering—through *equity*, i.e., the equality of outcome, and *so-*

---

[92] *Equity*. Oxford Learner's Dictionary. https://www.oxfordlearnersdictionaries.com/definition/english/equity_1?q=equity. Accessed 02/05/2022.
[93] Critical Race Training in Education. "What Is Critical Race Theory?" Legal Insurrection Foundation. 2022. https://criticalrace.org/what-is-critical-race-theory/. Accessed 01/25/2022.

cial justice, i.e., a vision where the distribution of re-sources is equitable.[94] Critical race theory is, unlike tradi-tional civil rights movements pushing for progress, to di-rectly question the very foundations of our society;[95] in other words, there is a revolution brewing in our midst. The Übermenschen have found their purpose!

The most reliable method to decipher the means by which equity and social justice are to be pushed, and the true goal that CRT has embedded into it, is to look back over the past. I am not the first to attempt such a feat,[96] nor will I be the last, but I am compelled to do so in my own way, for I fear for the future of our nation, and the West as a whole.

It is no secret that followers of the cult identify openly as Marxists in their doctrine, so that is where we must go, back to the cauldron in which it was concocted and the influence and impacts it has had in many different parts of the world.

---

[94] Brandeis University. "Diversity, Equity & Inclusion"—Social Justice. https://www.brandeis.edu/diversity/resources/definitions.html. Accessed 02/05/2022.
[95] Delgado, Richard. *Critical Race Theory: An Introduction.* NYU Press, 3rd edi-tion. March 7, 2017. p. 3
[96] Lindsay , James. "Critical Race Theory." New Discourses. Revised 11/14/2020. https://newdiscourses.com/tftw-critical-race-theory/. Accessed 02/05/2022.

The Inception of Marxism

It was Paris, the City of Light, which saw the beginnings of anticapitalist thought at the beginning of the nineteenth century. France had gone through its infamous revolution; Napoleon Bonaparte had failed to realize his dream of an empire larger than that of Charlemagne, which would consequently cripple France's ambition of territorial expansion. His warmongering led to the dissolution of the First French Republic, and the monarchy was reinstated in 1814. The Congress of Vienna ensured that the return of the Bourbon King Louis XVIII would bring about a constitution. The Charter of 1814 saw France adopt its very first constitution, and citizens witnessed the beginning of the shift of power from the crown to the people; France had become a constitutional monarchy. Industrialism had brought machinofacture to Western and Central Europe, and the widening chasm between the propertyless working people, the proletariat, and the bourgeoisie class, who owned land and factories, had exacerbated social sentiments. Workers were paid low wages, barely enough to survive, and lived in poor and unhealthy conditions, while the factory owners enjoyed lavish lifestyles.

This growing tension prompted many unorthodox speculators to gather in Paris, the hotbed of revolutionary impulses, to engage in discussion and debate on societal progress. Paris became the headquarters of many anticapitalist social theorists, who argued that the face of evil came not only from the unfair distribution of resources but also from individualism itself. "By means of economic planning, the gnawing tension of competition and all kinds of exploitation would cease," proclaimed Comte Henri de Saint-Simone (1760–1825). He was the pioneer of the utopian socialist school of thought, which was strongly against *laissez-fair* individualism. Saint-Simone came to the conclusion that for the proper study of humankind, one must focus not on the individual but on the masses. In an idyllic new age, he predicted that a group of scholarly scientists and socially dedicated technocrats would govern.

The teachings of the Comte resonated strongly with another rebel seeking to abolish low pay and horrid working conditions at the booming factories in France during the first half of the nineteenth century—François M. C. Fourier (1772–1837). He championed the creation of independent and self-sufficient communities, called *phalanstères*, a compound term from French *phalange* (phalanx) and *monastère* (monastery).[97] Those places would be free of the evils of machinofacture and the unfairness of capitalism. A federal union of such communities would replace the autocratic state. Each of those communities

---

[97] Harper, Douglas. *Phalanstery*. Online Etymology Dictionary. https://www.etymonline.com/word/phalanstery. Accessed 02/03/2022.

would house five hundred to two thousand people who would live in apartment blocks equipped with all amenities necessary for an isolated life (nurseries, communal dining, and lecture halls). Members would work the land and mills and practically produce all necessities of existence. Men and women would be able to switch jobs, and plenty of serene leisure would be available.

The regime of King Louis Philippe (reigned 1830–1848) had many intellectual adversaries. Suffrage was restricted to high tax-paying citizens, and his prime minister, François Guizot, contributed to the perversion of governmental institutions by corruption. [98] Firm resistance to reform and nostalgia for the glory days of Bonaparte inspired many republican and democratic thinkers to throw down the monarchy. A staunch opponent of the status quo was Étienne Cabet (1788–1856). He preached the radical ideas that there should be no private property, production ought to be planned by servants of the state, and citizen equality should even extend to the clothes that they wear. The young Louis Blanc (1811–1882) with his vivid anticapitalist doctrines, proved more popular with the low-paid workers. In his *L'Organisation du Travail* (*Organization of Labor*), he saw competition as the prime evil of a good society and that equality in wages must reign supreme. Pierre J. Proudhon (1809–1865), famously dubbed the "father of anarchism" in post-

---

[98] May, Arthur. *The Age of Metternich, 1814-1848*. Holt, Rinehart and Winston, Inc. Revised edition. 1963. p. 97.

Napoleonic France, bitterly proclaimed that "property is theft" in his scandalous *Qu'est-ce que la Propriété? (What Is Property?)*. He argued that private ownership benefitted a privileged few while keeping the masses in misery.

At the time that these assaults on capitalism were taking place, the Prussian-born Karl Marx (1818–1883) was the editor of the *Rheinische Zeitung* liberal newspaper, which he turned from cautious criticism of the Prussian government to open radical critique. Consequently, the newspaper was shut down, and Marx moved to bohemian Paris in 1843, where he studied utopian developments closely, borrowed from them, and began a close friendship with Friedrich Engels (1820–1895). Engels was Marx's most important intellectual collaborator.

The two worked tirelessly to spread their radical ideas among workers and intellectuals, which culminated in their most important publication—the *Communist Manifesto* of 1848. The year was marked by revolutions throughout continental Europe, save for the empire of the tsars, Russia, and Belgium. Sharp economic recession ravaged the continent in the late 1840s; riots and bloody encounters forced the French king Louis Philippe to abdicate in 1848. Hastily, aristocratic regimes were replaced by short-lived republican governments, only for the latter to collapse and allow the former to reassert themselves. Living and working conditions for the urban poor remained unchanged.

Marx's most profound anticapitalist argument was the eternal conflict between the bourgeois class and the proletariat, which was intrinsic to a capitalist society. The upper class lives in luxury and abundance. They control materials, capital, and machinery and exert oppression on the lower class. The working class lives in poverty with no security or prospects for the pursuit of personal wealth. He envisioned a world devoid of social classes, a society constituted by a free association of producers (a "cooperative" rather than individual control of economic resources)—a communist society. Such a society would devote itself to the free development and flourishing of individuals.

The gospel of Marx predicted that the toppling of capitalism by a socialist revolution was inevitable. Both Marx and Engels actively pressed for the implementation of and encouraged an organized proletarian revolution in order to abolish capitalism and achieve socio-economic emancipation. Unfortunately, they would not see the fruits of their labors materialize in their own lifetimes. Engels himself described Marx in a speech at Marx's grave as, above all, a fighter, a revolutionary who devoted his entire life to the liberation and emancipation of the modern proletariat.[99]

---

[99] Bailey, Andrew et al. *The Broadview Anthology of Social and Political Thought.* Vol I. Broadview Press. 2008. p. 983.

The Red Terror

Carl Marx and his ideological peers were highly influential in many European socialist movements, most of which existed briefly in the nineteenth century and gained little to no major support. However, their ideas were able to persevere because of the freedom and tolerance given by thriving liberalism in many European states.[100] It wasn't until the beginning of the twentieth century in tsarist Russia that communism gained a solid foothold in governmental affairs. Up to that point in history, the terms socialism and communism were synonymous and used interchangeably. Some socialist movements preferred a pacifist approach to bringing the social ideals into flourishing democratic capitalist societies through reformation rather than through revolution. Others were not so keen on this idea. Vladimir Ulyanov, also known as Lenin (1870–1924), is responsible for the creation of communism as we know it today. He declared that only through violent revolution can the proletariat state replace the bourgeois establishment. He rejected any notions that the masses would lead, as other socialist branches envisioned, and instead created a dictatorship of the state to lead the proletariat against democracy

---

[100] Salvadori, Massimo. *The Rise of Modern Communism: A Brief History of the Communist Movement in the Twentieth Century.* Henry Holt and Company, New York. 1952. p. 6.

and capitalism. There is to be only one political party made up of "elites" to control all social and economic life.[101]

Lenin's communist faction, known as the Bolsheviks, formed its own party in 1912. World War I proved highly advantageous to the Bolsheviks' aim of transforming the imperialistic war into a civil war against the bourgeoisie and Russia's autocratic government. On the night of October 24, 1917, the Bolshevik minority seized political power using military squads. Eight months later, it was evident that they favored little popular support, and in order to stay in power, they unleashed a reign of terror. All opposition, including liberals and anti-communists, were viciously liquidated.[102] The Russian Royal Romanov family was brutally murdered; the bodies of the tsar's family were dismembered and burned on gasoline-soaked pyres. Members of the extended family were thrown alive down a mining shaft and bombarded with hand grenades.[103] Up to one million "enemies of the people" were killed during this tumultuous event. Thus began the Communist regime of terror in the East, Marx's prophecy of the "dictatorship of the proletariat," in which the "elite" few forcibly took control of one of the largest countries in the world.

---

[101] Ibid. pp. 10-11.
[102] Ibid. p. 24.
[103] "Death at Ekaterinburg." *Time* magazine. 1935. https://web.archive.org/web/20080604141845/http://www.time.com/time/magazine/article/0,9171,762269-2,00.html. Accessed 03/13/2022.

The end of the Russian Civil War in 1922 marked the formation of the Union of Soviet Socialist Republics (USSR). The USSR nurtured its people into the belief that all are equal and that all shall get an equal share, or so the story is told by some who were born in the 1950s and 1960s in developing countries in the former Soviet sphere of influence. They did that by a system of economy that, on paper, was to ensure that there would be enough means to go around for everyone. Those who did not want to work were forced to because everyone had to give "according to his ability" their fair share. This they enforced by the so-called Brezhnev Doctrine, the Soviet Union's policy of intervention by military force, if necessary, to preserve Communist rule. In essence, to provide equity, one must take it by force from somebody else who has plenty and give it to those that don't have enough, through an artificial economy of surplus. The reign of terror of the communists had just begun in 1921. All industrial business was collectivized (nationalized), private ownership of homes was prohibited, peasants were forced to surrender most of their produce to the government, and the monetary system was replaced with a system of coupons.

Joseph Stalin (1879–1953), by eliminating his political opponents, took over leadership of the Communist party, and subsequently as a dictator of the Soviet Union, after Lenin's death in 1924. Stalin could be named a man as evil as Adolf Hitler (1889–1945), despite his alliance of necessity in WWII on the Allied side, with millions of deaths on his hands. Although the GULAG (in English, Main Administration of Corrective Labor Camps) was established by Lenin; Stalin employed them to the fullest. Criminals, political dissidents, undesirables, and recalcitrant citizens were sent to the GULAG to either correct through forced labor or be killed. Twelve to fourteen million people have passed through the five hundred GULAG facilities with no less than 1.5 million dead from 1930 to 1956.[104]

In the early years of utopia, the largest section of the population in the USSR was comprised of rich peasants (Kulaks—not "landowners," but farmers who still owned land, houses, and livestock), who preferred the socialist opposition. In 1930 Stalin and his accomplices in the Communist Party decided to eliminate the Kulaks because they were considered "hesitant" allies. So swift and efficient they were at this endeavor that in less than two months, about five million Kulaks either ended up in the GULAG or were shot, and their assets "collectivized."[105] Such brutality befell even prisoners of war: most of the soldiers of the Red Army who had been captured by the Nazis passed from the Nazi concentration camps

---

[104] Getty, Arch. Rittersporn, Gábor. Zemskov, Viktor. *Victims of the Soviet penal system in the pre-war years: a first approach on the basis of archival evidence.* American Historical Review. 1993. 98 (4): pp. 1017–1049. https://doi.org/10.2307/2166597 Accessed 05/25/2022
[105] Salvadori, Massimo. *The Rise of Modern Communism: A Brief History of the Communist Movement in the Twentieth Century.* Henry Holt and Company, New York. 1952. pp. 41-42.

straight into "the GULAG Archipelago" after Hitler's suicide.[106] Full nationalization of agriculture and state monopoly over education, the press, and all other forms of communication were instituted not only within the borders of the USSR but also its Eastern European "satellite states" as well, which were cast behind the Iron Curtain after WWII—Albania, Bulgaria, Romania, Yugoslavia, Poland, Czechoslovakia, Eastern Germany.[107]

Karl Kautsky (1854–1938), a close friend of Engels and later the German Social-Democratic Party leader, has made a resonating summary of the communist method: "The fundamental aim of the Communists of every country is not the destruction of capitalism but the destruction of democracy." The Soviet Union collapsed in 1991, smothered by the falsity of its own lies and bloodlust, its total opposition to democratic and humanistic values. Marxism has never touched the United States in any way close to how it has the European continent, but now it is showing signs of popular support in the form of racism theories, and that should disturb everyone. Our country was not founded on the communist principles of Marx and Engels. We hold democracy in the one hand and capitalism in the other. We believe in equal opportunities for all, not equal outcomes. Everyone is in charge of their

---

[106] Müller, Rolf-Dieter. Ueberschär Gerd. *Hitler's War in the East, 1941-1945: A Critical Assessment.* Berghahn Books. Second Revised Edition. 2002. p. 219.
[107] Salvadori, Massimo. *The Rise of Modern Communism: A Brief History of the Communist Movement in the Twentieth Century.* Henry Holt and Company, New York. 1952. p. 68.

own destinies. The United States of America remains the land of endless opportunities for those who have the ambition to make something of themselves. Those who give their best effort will reap the rewards. Those who sit and whine in self-pitying infantilism, begging that their government take complete care of them, will not. Meritocracy is what is practically achievable and just. The *I* is the smith of one's own future.

"Those who do not know history are doomed to repeat it," said Edmund Burke (1729–1797), by succumbing to an old record, an old utopia under a new name and pretenses—critical race theory and all of its partners in crime. Like Marx before them, they seek to overthrow the status quo by exploiting racial conflict or what little there is; if there isn't any, then they must create it!

A Wolf Among Sheep

*Let the ruling classes tremble at a Communistic
revolution. The proletarians have nothing to lose
but their chains. They have a world to win.*

—Karl Marx, *The Communist Manifesto*

So brutal was the legacy of Marx and Engels, and it,
unfortunately, lives on in some places of the world.
It is a true tragedy that the yoke of communism still
endures after almost a full century in Russia and half a
century throughout the rest of Eastern Europe. Now, let
us return to the subject of racism theories. A rather late
distinction must here be made that for the purposes of
analyzing the Marxist nature of race theories, we may use
the term Marxism interchangeably with communism. Socialism and communism are both rooted in Marxism;
however socialism, as we mentioned earlier, calls for
peaceful reform and envisions a somewhat democratic
form of governing, while communism invokes a bloody
and global revolution, the goal of which is totalitarian-
ism with a despot at the helm.

Both the Modern Racism Scale and Implicit Association Test suffer from the same deficiencies as the theories they are based on: they are prone to a high amount of false positives and false negatives; they have not shown to undoubtedly measure subconscious racism, and consequently and most importantly, they cannot predict real-world behavior.[108] They are impossible to refute and also impossible to prove,[109] which puts them undeniably outside the category of science-fact.

Previously we alluded to the question of the quantification of racism. As far as modern racism and critical race theories are concerned with the matter, the short answer is that there is no reliable scientific way to measure racism. In fact, modern racism and critical race theories cannot in any way imaginable be called *a priori* truths, as they severely lack empirical evidence. All these theories can present in their defense are statistical probabilities, inferences, assumptions, and an amount of literature dedicated to this new obsession to make your head spin.

To give the charge that all American institutions are inherently racist some credibility, it must be measurably

---

[108] Nagai, Althea. "The Implicit Association Test: Flawed Science Tricks Americans into Believing They Are Unconscious Racists." 2017. https://www.heritage.org/science-policy/report/the-implicit-association-test-flawed-science-tricks-americans-believing-they. Accessed 02/05/2022.
[109] Bartlett, Tom. "Can We Really Measure Implicit Bias? Maybe Not." *Chronicle of Higher Education.* 01/05/2017. https://www.chronicle.com/article/can-we-really-measure-implicit-bias-maybe-not/. Accessed 02/05/2022.

demonstrable,[110] which inadvertently leads to the introduction of a new psychological construct. We have made
a leap of faith from pure or theoretical racism, a phenomenon clearly defined within our legal frameworks, to an
illusive and subjectively quantifiable variant called *perceived* racism. If one cannot successfully argue in a court
of law that an act of discrimination or a manifestation of
racism in the physical universe has occurred, then one
must argue that the hand of the law should be guided by
the feelings of the wounded party. Perception is purely
the result of one's senses, i.e., feelings. Following this line
of thinking, we may as well conclude that we perceive a
notion that racism could be quantified as an internal,
psychological condition and not a directly measurable
phenomenon to warrant a crusade of social justice warriors. For all intents and purposes, it is safe for us to agree
with the widely accepted notion that racism (as we know
it from history books) no longer exists in America, and to
refuse to believe in nonsense.

  Like its predecessors, CRT remains a theory and not
a proven fact; it cannot at the moment produce any such
empirical evidence to prove that institutions, and subsequently white people in general, are inherently racist. If
CRT has not been proven, then its contents are nothing
more than beliefs, beliefs which it has already begun

---

[110] Atkins, Rahshida. "Instruments Measuring Perceived Racism/Racial Discrimination: Review and Critique of Factor Analytic Techniques." *International Journal of Health Service.* 2014. https://jour-
nals.sagepub.com/doi/10.2190/HS.44.4.c. Accessed 02/05/2022.

spreading like the tentacles of an octopus. Let us see for ourselves how the iron hand of social justice is seeking to turn our democracy upside down.

Assault on the Family

A mind-blowing piece of news came out of Australia[iii] in 2015 regarding two philosophers, Adam Swift and Harry Brighouse. They've landed on the realization that being raised in a caring and well-off family gives the child an unfair advantage over other children. What's more, it isn't just about your family being able to afford private schooling, nannies, tutors, and a house in a good neighborhood; it is that functional family interactions form invisible but substantial fault lines between families. Swift's solution from an "instrumental" standpoint to the social justice problem is to simply abolish the family. However, in order not to be perceived as someone from antiquity (Plato entertained the same idea in his *Republic* even though his work is interpreted with an eye of a metaphysical nature), he concedes that there is too much value in the family to just be tossed to the flames, and to let our children grow up in phalanstère-style education facilities. The Chinese communists would not be alone with their "(re)education" camps full of Uyghur minorities.

Having figured out that nobody in their right mind would relinquish full and total control of their children to

---

[iii] Galonesi, Joe. "Is Having a Loving Family an Unfair Advantage?" https://www.abc.net.au/radionational/programs/philosopherszone/new-family-values/6437058. May 1, 2015. Accessed 1/30/2022.

the state (or whoever it is that would ensure a fair up-
bringing . . . perhaps little "servants of the state"), Swift
and Brighouse have come up with a laundry list of things
which parents shouldn't be allowed to do in order to prevent unfairness to other people's children. In their view,
both bedtime stories and elite private schools bestow advantage, but again, it would be unthinkable to forbid parents to read bedtime stories to their children. However,
limiting or outright banning private schools would be fair
game.

Another outlandish, and at the same time grandiose
synthesis of high communist thought, is to impose limita-
tions on inheritance. Inheritance is an economic means
of conferring advantage, they argue. Equity, as we've discovered earlier, is the final destination of the struggling
"classes," or in this case, races. Their ultimate emancipation and their ability to develop freely their individual
selves will be accomplished when all are nothing but
equal. Never mind how boring the world would be where
all humans wear the same clothes, drive the same cars,
own exact-looking houses, speak the same language, and
get paid the same amount of wages; we cannot possibly
allow them to pass down and receive inheritance—that
would be sacrilege! "Property is theft!" Does it not then
follow that if inheritance wouldn't be passed down, one
wouldn't own any property? Otherwise, what would be
the purpose of owning property if one cannot pass it
down to their heirs? The almighty Social Justice Deity

will not allow private property, just like the Soviets did not!

It is so refreshing to know that somebody took Plato's foundational work of the Tripartite Soul Theory (*Republic*), turned the paradigm into a parody by giving it a literal interpretation, and tried to apply it to the modern world full of struggle, racism, unfairness, and inequity. In Plato's idyllic utopia, everybody would have a role (three roles he assigned to everyone—ruling, working, and enforcing), and societies would be governed by philosophers.[112] Those would-be philosophers are to be found at an early age and nurtured to rule wisely and fairly, but nobody else would be able to switch their roles. One can't possibly go from a philosopher to a "worker" or vice-versa without the gift: the gift, which is bestowed by the gods of fairness and social justice. They are to grab the universe by its horns and bring order to chaos, plenty to little, and fairness to inequity.

Consequently, the global social justice cult is trying to convince us that we should be proud to lose our liberties by being raised the exact same way as everybody else and to have no ability to possess individual property—all in the name of a fair and equitable society!

Isn't it logical to suppose that fairness and equality of outcome are impossible to achieve for the simple fact that nobody is born equal? For one, we have different ge-

---

[112] Plato. *Republic*. 368a-376c.

netics. Many would disagree with this and say that analysis of the human genome shows that all humans share 99.9 percent of genetic material, and yet there is the 0.01 percent that makes us different! We also all have different family backgrounds and intellectual capacities. Like it or not, 7.8 billion people don't possess the exact same IQ, and 7.8 billion people will never be made to possess the exact same IQ. Equality of opportunity is a goal within closer reach.

Now, let me pose a few sets of questions. Why dwell on this existential dilemma of equal opportunity versus equal outcome? What if we removed opportunity from the question? Why is equality within the context of outcome so important? What is the driving force for someone to want to be the same (equal) as somebody else? Could it be as simple as being as compassionate and generous as to want others to have what you have? Or is it a manifestation of the irrational child within us, driven by impulses, who wants the same things which his peers possess? Or could it be any combination of envy, jealousy, or anger?

Did Marx not say himself that everybody should realize their full potential? Wouldn't that include personal wealth? If everybody is to be paid the same, what is your personal wealth compared to somebody else's wealth? Is it still wealth if both people have the same amount and nothing else to compare it to?

Critical (E)race Doctrine

The doctrine of the anti-racist crusaders has crept up in our schools. The term *doctrine* is appropriate, as it describes the next piece of the puzzle—indoctrination. It starts with the simple principle that all institutions are inherently racist, including our educational system. In order to weed racism out of our schools, the process of indoctrination is employed. It is the process of circumventing reasoning in order to impart a specific way of thinking based on something other than evidence, so that the child (and adults included) holds beliefs irrationally, with no regard for empirical evidence. [113] By bypassing rationale, reason, and proof, indoctrination imparts beliefs by exerting psychological pressure,[114] much like Islamic extremism.

The Nazis in pre-WWII Germany employed indoctrination, and so did the Bolsheviks in the Soviet Union, Mussolini's fascists in Italy, and China's Mao comrades. What these four vile factions had in common was fundamentalism: an unwavering attachment to a set of irreducible beliefs and virtues, and consequent rejection of diversity of opinion. There is no room for rationalism

---

[113] Cuevas, Joshua. "The Psychological Processes and Consequences of Fundamentalist Indoctrination." Equinox Publishing Ltd. 2013. p. 58. https://journals.equinoxpub.com/index.php/EPH/article/view/17689. Accessed 02/05/2022.

[114] Ibid.

amidst the cesspool of fundamentalism. In order to put rejection into practice, Hitler, Stalin, Mussolini, and Mao had to enforce their doctrines on the population who disagreed by rooting out all enemies of the people. That would ensure that future generations would comply by launching thought reform campaigns, i.e., propagandist pedagogy. They did not want an Average Joe capable of critical thinking, reasoning, and rationale; they wanted obedient workers who wouldn't question their perverted ideals.

CRT was conceived in an academic environment and riddled with much pseudo- and nowhere-near-pseudo-scientific mumbo-jumbo. Its grip is greatest and its impact felt the hardest in educational institutions. It is of no surprise that so many protests by parents have been taking place at K–12 schools across the country to oppose CRT being shoved down their children's throats. Let us go on an expedition and discover what it is that public schools are accused of forcing on children.

The Legal Insurrection Foundation's website by the name Critical Race Training in Education, in its "What Is Critical Race Theory?" page,[115] lists nine different ways that colleges and universities have responded to the increased demands by activists to take anti-racist actions. Those actions include making the admissions process

---

[115] Critical Race Training in Education. "What Is Critical Race Theory?" Legal Insurrection Foundation. 2022. https://criticalrace.org/what-is-critical-race-theory/. Accessed 02/08/2022.

more *equitable*, implementing training to help students and staff understand their *implicit biases*, embedding anti-racist *ideology* in class materials, political anti-racist *activism* support in monetary form (donations to Black Lives Matter), funding CRT programs and research, disarming or *defunding* university police departments, offering anti-racist resources, etc. The website also has a list of colleges and universities that have subscribed to the CRT dogma in one way or another and also keeps track of the steps that those schools have taken or intend to take. It is staggering to realize how far higher education institutions have gone to push for an equitable and anti-racist society through activism and defunding of the police. That is the source of the blissful insight, the eye-opening realization, and sudden awakening that the world needs correcting—an indoctrinating academic environment[116]— and through it, all shall kneel before the CRT king, basking in his equitable radiance. Credit must be given, however, where it is due. The website on its "K–12" page[117] does state that the Legal Insurrection Foundation's primary aim is not to propagate CRT into K–12 schools and recognizes the controversy that CRT is causing in primary and secondary schools.

Our journey takes us to the state of Oregon next. Like many public schools throughout the country, Tigard-

---

[116] Duchesne, Ricardo. *Faustian Man in a Multicultural Age*. Arktos Media Ltd. 2017. pp. 194-195.
[117] Critical Race Training in Education. "K-12." Legal Insurrection Foundation. 2022. https://criticalrace.org/k-12/. Accessed 02/08/2022.

Tualatin School District in Oregon (TTSD), through a resolution,[118] has embraced the practice of "Diversity, Equity, Inclusion." The most important points to our field of inquiry are thus (with my emphases):

1. They pledge to "be actively *anti-racist* and *dismantle systemic racism*" in their schools and "empower people of color."[119] The terms *anti-racist* and *dismantling of systemic racism*, quite familiar to us by now, suggest deep devotion to the CRT, and ultimately, the anti-American cult.

2. They "affirm the value and importance of *culturally responsive pedagogy*." Perhaps they mean to insert the process of understanding one's own implicit biases?

3. They "commit to using an *equity lens* for all future curriculum adoptions." The Marxist ideal is to be pushed in its latest incarnation—equity.

TTSD is not the only school district in the country to have gone woke. Buffalo Public Schools are now actively recruiting students in the Black Lives Matter movement[120] and are committed to disrupting the "Western-prescribed nuclear family structure."[121] San Diego Unified

[118] Wolf, Maureen. "Resolution 1920-19 of the Tigard-Tualatin School Board of Directors." Tigard-Tualatin School District. 06/08/2020. https://www.ttsdschools.org/Page/9770. Accessed 02/05/20202.
[119] Ibid.
[120] Buffalo Public Schools. "Black Lives Matter Curriculum." 2020. https://www.buffaloschools.org/Page/93603. Accessed 02/09/2022.
[121] Buffalo Public Schools. "5th Grade: Black Lives Matter." Office of Culturally and Linguistically Responsive Initiatives. 2020. https://www.buffaloschools.org/cms/lib/NY01913551/Centricity/Domain/9000/BLM%20lesson%20-%20Grade%205.pdf. Accessed 02/09/2022.

School District decided to be an anti-racist school district and abolish the "discriminatory grading practices" which they saw by comparing the failing grades of the black (20 percent) versus white (7 percent) students.[122] Another example worthy of mention is how anonymous student activists, Black at UNIS, at New York's elite United Nations International School, threatened a "policy of no mercy" in order to force the school into the anti-racism worldview.[123] Anti-racist activism among students has already begun turning into terrorism.

The cult has infiltrated our education system. Through culturally responsive teaching (*erase* your own whiteness) and equity curriculums (the lazy and the hard-working must get the same economic outcome), the cult is indoctrinating children into activists, revolutionaries, and social justice warriors. It is embedded in their ideology that the current system must burn, and from the ashes, a new world shall arise, one free from racism, inequity, discrimination, and pathological whiteness. At what cost, may I ask? If the deadly protests in Minneapolis, Portland, Kenosha, Chicago, Houston, and many other cities are any indication, it is that the cultists are commit-

[122] Rowe, Ian. "The Soft Bigotry of Anti-Racist Expectations Is Damaging to Black and White Kids Alike." *USA Today*. 2020. https://www.usatoday.com/story/opinion/2020/12/06/anti-racism-lowering-expectations-education-just-form-soft-bigotry-column/6410954002/. Accessed 02/09/2022.
[123] Rufo, Christopher. "Spoiled Rotten." *City Journal*. 2021. https://www.cityjournal.org/black-at-unis-campaign. Accessed 02/09/2022.

ted to the cause and ready for a revolution, an anti-Western revolution. What other definition is there for the destruction caused and lives lost during those "peaceful protests," as some news outlets insisted on portraying them? For eighty-three consecutive nights in 2020, mobs of BLM supporters wreaked havoc on downtown Portland, Oregon, vandalizing businesses and local and federal government buildings.[124] The unrest in Minneapolis, Minnesota, resulted in seven hundred buildings being damaged, with at least twelve completely destroyed by protesters who terrorized the city.[125] Residents of the small city of Kenosha, Wisconsin saw one hundred businesses looted and damaged, with at least forty decimated to piles of rubble.[126] Let us also not forget the catastrophic death toll caused by the Antifa and BLM terror in 2020 . . .

No revolution has passed through the pages of history without violence and bloody murder. Unless the vile octopus gets its tentacles severed in our school systems,

[124] Brown, Lee. "Portland Businesses Fleeing Downtown Offices Over Nightly BLM Riots." *NY Post.* 08/19/2020. https://nypost.com/2020/08/19/portland-businesses-fleeing-downtown-over-nightly-blm-riots/. Accessed 05/27/2022.
[125] CBS Minnesota. "Minneapolis Issues Map Showing Extent of Buildings Damaged in Unrest Over George Floyd's Death." 06/16/2020. https://minnesota.cbslocal.com/2020/06/16/minneapolis-issues-map-showing-extent-of-buildings-damaged-in-unrest-over-george-floyds-death/. Accessed 05/27/2022.
[126] McAdams, Alexis. "Kenosha Unrest Damages More Than 100 Buildings, at Least 40 Destroyed, Alliance Says." WLS-TV. 09/02/2020. https://abc7chicago.com/kenosha-shooting-protest-looting-fires/6402998/. Accessed 05/27/2022.

our own children may be part of this bloody revolution. It is, however, through constructive and rational discourse that the cult must be banished; if we're to fight hate with hate, then we, those who possess a sliver of rational thinking, are no better than them.

Anti-Racist Terror

Parents across the country have been taking up the fight in protest against school boards' intent to implement CRT curriculums, training, and equity programs, and they are facing a formidable adversary. The anti-racists organize online and encourage the recording, exposing, and shaming of anti-CRT parents.[127] The anti-racists are to take photos of license plates and speeches made by their enemies at school board meetings; they are to *hiss* when "outsiders" are speaking. They are told to search the very depths of the Internet to find who the racists are and then to contact their employers and any organizations they are part of to be publicly shamed and stoned (not literally, but by being fired from their jobs) for daring to speak against anti-racism.

The cult activists use the terms *racist* and *white supremacist* interchangeably.[128] Their enemies cannot be surveyed via Implicit Association Test or Modern Racism Scale and assigned an unconscious racism score to assess the magnitude of their inherent racism. This is because anyone who opposes their ideals is automatically

---

[127] Zaveleta, Raul. "The Indoctrination of Our Children." Corpus Christi for Unity and Peace. 2021. https://www.corpuschristiforunityandpeace.org/the-indoctrination-of-our-children/. Accessed 02/01/2022.
[128] Ibid.

considered an enemy. There are only racist and anti-racist,[129] and nothing in between. Their ideology does not provide a spectrum on which to place members of society—one is either with the cult or against it.

The Order of Social Justice is spiteful; it retaliates by a tactic all too familiar to us in this day and age—cancel culture. The members of the Order are encouraged to coerce through intimidation and canceling. If you show up to a protest, your employer must be notified and have you released from employment; any and all organizations you are a part of must cut you out like the cancer that you are on society. You must be shamed publicly, lynched psychologically and economically until you break and embrace their truth. The Terror of the Woke shall rule! The mob of angry social justice warriors who in order to fix a few perceived injustices create many more tangible injustices—burning, looting, murdering. Those are the labors of Marxism, the reality of communism, the aspirations of the Woke, the true purpose of the Eternal Victim. In a country where civil liberties for all are the norm, the Eternal Victim must become an oppressor—to throw down merit and install equity. One needn't have a PhD to see the ugly face of truth.

---

[129] Ferlazzo, Larry. "Educators Must Realize That There Is No Neutral Position on Issues of Racial Justice." *EducationWeek*. 2020. https://www.edweek.org/teaching-learning/opinion-educators-must-realize-that-there-is-no-neutral-position-on-issues-of-racial-justice/2020/06?cmp=soc-edit-tw. Accessed 02/08/2022.

In the end, it is safe to deduce that CRT cannot even be called a theory; a theory does not incite or condone violence, intimidation, or canceling. That is the job of propaganda, propaganda so heinous that it terrorizes its adversaries into submission or obliteration. After all, nobody would test the premises of CRT if everyone believed it to be valid. Schools are places where our descendants are to learn how to think for themselves, through evidence-based inquiry and rational argumentation, not through Marxist and anti-Western propaganda masquerading as social justice, rooted in hate, rage, and envy, the ethos of the infantile Eternal Victim.

All revolutions begin in educated circles. The intellectuals who support and fight for a cause rally the masses, and then the revolution takes place. Marx and Engels collaborated for most of their lives to spread their radical philosophy; Engels took part in a failed military uprising in 1848 as an officer;[130] they were both tried in court in Cologne for inciting revolt and exiled to England where they continued their communist cause. Will history repeat itself and bring justice upon those who incite hate and violence in our cities in our day and age? Will anyone be held accountable for the carnage and destruction across the country led by various anti-racist groups in 2020? Let's keep telling ourselves that it's for a good cause and that the social justice cult is mostly peaceful . . .

---

[130] Bailey, Andrew et al. *The Broadview Anthology of Social and Political Thought.* Vol I. Broadview Press. 2008. p. 982.

A Nation Divided

Despite the media's best efforts to portray the Antifa and BLM protests of 2020 as mostly peaceful, even the Legal Insurrection website, an outlet of the Legal Insurrection Foundation, has a much different outlook on reality.[131] But what did one expect to happen, I wonder, when one incites the masses of unsophisticated simpletons to take the law into their own hands and to do justice? How do the acts of burning, looting, and murdering bring justice? Is burning down a police station going to bring justice to George Floyd? Is the looting of department stores and local businesses going to bring Breonna Taylor back? *O sancta simplicitas!* An ignoramus can be nothing but an ignoramus. An ignoramus is not the kind of person who is intelligent and simply unfamiliar with certain topics. It is the person who is unsophisticated by nature and throughout his or her life gains no insight into the humanities, a person who the humanities are unable to tame and civilize, who contributes nothing of value to society, a simpleton, a philistine, a lout, a slob. The ignoramus is given strength and courage by the backing of Antifa and BLM by corporate America as another form

---

[131] Mathews, Stacey. "Flashback 2020: Six Months of Antifa/BLM Looting, Rioting, and Chaos." Legal Insurrection. 01/09/2021. https://legalinsurrection.com/2021/01/flashback-2020-six-months-of-antifa-blm-looting-rioting-and-chaos/. Accessed 05/27/2022.

of advertising for them, a game of return on investment. It's in style to be anti-racist, and so anti-racists will buy their products, which in turn will make their corporate accomplices higher profits.

It is when the masses of ignorami revolt that glorious revolutions are carried out. The last queen of France, Marie Antoinette (1755–1793), was a misunderstood pioneer in her country of marriage, where she sought to set an example of womanhood in politics.[132] She found herself on the guillotine at the Place du Carrousel (formerly Place de la Révolution) in front of a swarm of French peasants in what was to be a fair trial.[133] The last tsar of Russia, Nicholas II (1868–1918), was a well-intentioned man canonized as a saint by the Russian Orthodox Church a decade after the fall of the Soviets. He, along with his wife Alexandra Feodorovna (1872–1918) and their five children, were bayoneted and dismembered by drunken Bolshevik peasants in the middle of the night without a trial, without mercy, leaving a room of carnage and smoke from the numerous gunshots.[134] Glorious indeed are the deeds of revolutionaries! Both democracy and communism have had their fair share of bloodshed

---

[132] Rady, Martin. *The Habsburgs: To Rule the World.* Basic Books. 2020. pp. 217-218.

[133] Fraser, Antonia. *Marie Antoinette: The Journey.* Nan A. Talese. 2001. pp. 424-425.

[134] Massie, Robert. *The Romanovs: The Final Chapter.* Random House Trade Paperbacks. 1996. pp. 3-6.

on their hands. What democratic and communist revolutions have in common is that somebody of certain intelligence organized the bloody acts. It takes somebody of intellectual sophistication to stir the masses of intellectual unsophistication to uprise and accomplish a glorious change. What the January 6 storming of the US Capitol did not have in common with the French and Bolshevik revolutions is that there was no glory in it. It was nothing but a farce, a charade orchestrated by ignorami for ignorami, a disgrace, another symptom of the cancer that has grown in the heart of our nation. It served no purpose other than to send a message to America that the far-right cultists are just as united in their ignorance as are the far left. Both camps have proven to be anything but glorious and nothing but pathetic.

It is the gravest sign of the decadence of our society when the vulgarity and philistinism become most obvious from the lowest citizen to the head of state. Such is the world that we live in today. The dormant flames of the Shadow archetype have been kindled, the beast has been unleashed, our barbarous selves are thirsty for blood and destruction. Two teams have emerged and engaged in a biblical battle of demons versus angels, an eternal conflict of extremism. Never mind that each is one side of the same coin, an atom violently split in two and one which will lay waste to the universe in its inevitable synthesis. The far left is just as insolent as the far right; both are unrelenting and unmovable in their convictions. Such a state of extreme polarization is, of course, convenient for the blue and red teams: a divided nation is a nation easy to rule. *Divide ut regnes!*

What fate is to befall us in the middle, us that see reason and work for meaningful progress, peace, and prosperity? We are mired in fog, invisible, disregarded, and cast aside, fighting a losing battle with the fury of the pendulum, ever taunted to pick a victor: the side of madness or the side of barbarism. We are the wounded party; we are the ones who truly suffer the consequences of the infantile pretenses of the ignorami, the burning and looting of our businesses, and the murdering of our children. We are the underrepresented whispers, the silent echoes in the ears of career politicians and wealthy tax-evading corporate criminals. We are the true majority, the backbone of this country, the mortified tax-paying bystander without whom there would be no police budget to defund, no corporate profits to split, no tax rates to slash, no money for welfare programs, no bright future to look forward to. What should happen if we are to revolt when the burden of existence becomes too heavy to bear? History may hold the answer.

Epilogue

We live in a free country, which we have the power to shape. Hate is not a beneficial force to invite into our private and public lives. Violence only creates pain and suffering.

Let us ascend, my dear citizens, into the decent beings we can be on this earth. Let us all show a little responsibility toward ourselves, others, and Mother Nature. Let us all be a little more understanding of each other and treat everyone with dignity and respect. Let us show a bit more humility and try to be more patient. And most importantly, let us spend less time on social media and more time face-to-face with loved ones and the outdoors.

It is as Kant said, that the humanities are what tame and civilize man, so let me make a few more propositions about our ascension. It would be more beneficial for all of us to spend more time with history, philosophy, and literature, the fine works of the great masters, and the spectacles of opera and theater.

Let us advance the American cause that our forefathers prescribed without hate, anger, and needless bloodshed. Let us march forward with open hearts and keep the American dream alive. God bless America!

www.ingramcontent.com/pod-product-compliance
Lightning Source LLC
Chambersburg PA
CBHW070723130626
46553CB00005B/2116